Editor
Mary S. Jones, M.A.

Illustrator
Kelly McMahon

Cover Artist
Brenda DiAntonis

Editor in Chief
Ina Massler Levin, M.A.

Creative Director
Karen J. Goldfluss, M.S. Ed.

Art Coordinator
Renée Christine Yates

Imaging
Leonard P. Swierski

Publisher

Mary D. Smith, M.S. Ed.

Prepare & **for** **STANDARDIZED TESTS** **Grade 2**

TCR 2892

M000165159

LANGUAGE ARTS

MATH

SOCIAL STUDIES

SCIENCE

Includes Standards

Includes a variety of strategies for successful test taking

Offers helpful tips and suggestions to reduce test anxiety

Teacher Created Resources

Author

Julia McMeans, M.Ed.

Teacher Created Resources, Inc.
6421 Industry Way
Westminster, CA 92683
www.teachercreated.com

ISBN: 978-1-4206-2892-0

© 2009 Teacher Created Resources, Inc.
Made in U.S.A.

Teacher Created Resources

Table of Contents

> Sentences—Sight Words—Types of Sentences—End Marks—Short and Long Vowels—Subjects
> and Predicates—Sentence Combining—Beginning Sounds—Ending Sounds—Parts of Speech—
> Letter Blends—Plural Nouns—Digraphs—Possessives—Synonyms—Antonyms—Adverbs and
> Adjectives—Proofing Sentences—Contractions—Friendly Letter—Silent Letters—Verb Tense—
> Reading Comprehension

> Place Value—Number Sense—Two-Digit Addition and Subtraction—Three-Digit Addition
> and Subtraction—Identifying Numbers—Counting Money—Problem Solving with Money—
> Geometry—Measurement—Time—Data

> Space—Fossils—Plants—Animals—Earth Science—Weather—Motion, Magnets, and
> Electricity—Matter—Heat, Sound, and Light—Human Body

> Earth's Features—Map Skills—Government—Our Country—Communities—Geography—
> U.S. History—Resources

> Reading—Math—Writing

Introduction

Standardized tests have not only been the subject of intense controversy among educators, but also the cause of much teeth gnashing among students. If individuals are unique, and learning styles and ways of understanding vary, how then can a standardized test accurately measure what a student knows?

There is a story of a first-grade teacher who held up a red apple to her class of 30 eager students and asked, "What color is this apple?" Twenty-nine of the students replied, "It's red," while one brave soul countered, "It's red and white." "Oh," the teacher responded, "I don't see any white," to which the student replied, "That's because you have to bite it!"

This is a cautionary tale that demonstrates that there are multiple ways in which to know, and that they can all potentially be correct. For this reason, it is critical that both educators and students understand what standardized tests seek to measure and the best strategies to prepare for and take these kinds of tests.

The vast majority of standardized tests that students encounter during their academic careers—including the California Achievement Test, the Iowa Test, and the Stanford Achievement Test—are norm-referenced tests. Norm-referenced tests compare and rank students in a particular grade with other students in that same grade. By doing this, educators can get a quick snapshot of where their students stand and to what extent their scores deviate from the average or the norm.

The content contained on standardized tests is aligned with state-wide curriculum standards, and vice versa. If a skill set appears in your content standards, it is reasonable to expect that it may appear on a standardized test. For example, you will never find a problem such as this on a second-grade standardized test: $4x - 3 = 17$.

However, you would very likely find a problem like this: $263 + 459$.

The reason is clear—basic algebra is not part of the second-grade core content for math, while the addition of three-digit numbers is.

It is imperative that students understand how standardized tests are scored, what they measure, and the kind of material they will encounter. By sharing this behind-the-scenes aspect of standardized tests with your students, you will help to empower them by demystifying the tests themselves, thus reducing the high anxiety often associated with them.

Standardized tests can be an effective measurement tool. Over the years, great steps have been taken not only to improve standardized testing—for instance, paying particular attention to bias in order to create tests that are more equitable—but also to provide students with an array of strategies that they can use in test-taking situations.

The purpose of this book is to help educators and students prepare for standardized tests by providing general information on test-taking strategies, tips on stress and anxiety reduction, and a variety of practice tests that span the core content that appears on these types of tests.

The practice tests contained within this book are arranged according to content area and then to specific skill sets within that area. The test questions are written in the style most frequently used on standardized tests and are aligned with the McREL Compendium of Content Standards.

McREL Compendium of Content Standards and Skills Index

Content Area	Standards Covered	Specific Skills Covered
R E A D I N G	• Uses the general skills and strategies of the reading process • Uses reading skills and strategies to understand and interpret a variety of literary texts	Sentences • Sight Words • Types of Sentences • Punctuation • Short and Long Vowels •Subjects and Predicates • Sentence Combining • Beginning Sounds • Ending Sounds • Parts of Speech • Blends • Plural Nouns • Digraphs • Possessives • Synonyms • Antonyms • Adverbs and Adjectives • Proofing • Sentences • Contractions • Letter Writing • Silent Letters • Verb Tense • Reading Comprehension
M A T H	• Uses a variety of strategies in the problem-solving process • Understands and applies basic and advanced properties of the concepts of numbers • Uses basic and advanced procedures while performing the processes of computation • Understands and applies basic and advanced properties of the concepts of measurement • Understands and applies basic and advanced properties of the concepts of geometry • Understands and applies basic and advanced properties of the concepts of statistics and data analysis • Understands and applies basic and advanced properties of functions and algebra	Place Value • Identifying Numbers • Addition • Subtraction • Writing Numbers • Money • Time • Problem Solving • Geometry • Measurement • Data

McREL Compendium of Content Standards and Skills Index

Content Area	Standards Covered	Specific Skills Covered
S C I E N C E	• Understands atmospheric processes and the water cycle • Understands Earth's composition and structure • Understands the composition and structure of the universe • Understands the structure and function of cells and organisms • Understands the relationship among organisms and their physical environments • Understands biological evolution and the diversity of life • Understands the structure and properties of matter • Understands the sources and properties of energy • Understands forces and motion	Solar System • Fossils • Plants • Animals • Rocks • Weather • Electricity • Motion • Magnets • Matter • Heat • Sound • Light • Human Body
H I S T O R Y and G E O G R A P H Y	• Understands family life now and in the past, and family life in various places long ago • Understands the history of a local community and how communities in North America varied long ago • Understands how democratic values came to be, and how they have been exemplified by people, events, and symbols • Understands the characteristics and uses of maps, globes, and other geographic tools and technologies • Knows the location of places, geographic features, and patterns of the environment • Understands the physical and human characteristics of place	Earth's Features and Landforms • Map Skills • Government • Communities • World Geography • United States History • Resources

General Test-Taking Strategies

Many things influence a student's performance on a standardized test—some are obvious, while others are elusive. Also, there are many factors over which educators have control, while there are many others over which they do not. Until someone invents a magic wand, word, or potion that can be waved over, said to, or imbibed by students, educators will have to rely on more conventional methods to help their students succeed on standardized tests. Below is a list of some general test-taking strategies with which students should be familiar.

1. Get a good night's sleep the night before the test. Most people need about eight hours.

2. Avoid caffeinated or other sugary drinks before taking the test, as they can make you jittery.

3. Eat a balanced breakfast.

4. Wear comfortable clothing.

5. Read or listen to the directions carefully. If something is unclear, ask for clarification.

6. Find out the rules of the test.

7. If you get stuck on a question, mark it and move on. You can come back to it later.

Reducing Test Anxiety

Anxiety can be debilitating in a test-taking situation, but it is important to remember that not all students experience test anxiety. There is a story about a first-year teacher who entered his room on test day and said jokingly to his seventh-grade class, "Well, is everybody nervous?" A student raised his hand and replied, "I'm nervous that I'm not nervous!"

Some students experience test anxiety, while others do not. And there are students for whom tests occasion a modicum of anxiety that not only does not inhibit their performance, but actually enhances it! The type of test anxiety we are concerned with here is the kind that severely impedes a student's ability to perform on a standardized test. But how do you know when a student has this kind of anxiety? There are several behaviors that might tip you off, including the following:

- Tardiness on test day
- Absenteeism on test day
- Crying
- Hyperactivity
- Lethargy
- Jitteriness
- Shallow breathing
- Sweating
- Nausea
- Muscle tension
- Distractibility
- Inability to focus

Of course, one of the biggest clues of test anxiety is when a student who demonstrates knowledge and understanding of content via his/her daily classroom performance falls apart when confronted with a standardized test that assesses the same skills.

Fortunately, there are a variety of strategies that can be taught to students suffering from test anxiety that can help them manage it. These strategies, however, should be routinely practiced by students in order for them to be effective. There is very little point in modeling positive self-talk five minutes before a test and then expecting that it will be of any use.

A Note to the Test Givers

Students are not the only people who experience test anxiety. Teachers, administrators, and other school personnel responsible for administering standardized tests can also experience anxiety around test time as pressure to increase student achievement mounts. While this is understandable, it is important to remember that anxiety is contagious: Anxious educators can often, inadvertently, create anxious students. Be mindful of your demeanor when administering the test. Create a relaxed, positive environment. Smile and maintain your sense of humor. Know that you have done your best to prepare your students. And your best is all that you can do!

Strategies for Reducing Test Anxiety

The following pages contain some of the most effective strategies available to help elementary, middle, high school, and even college students overcome test anxiety. By familiarizing students with all of these strategies and providing opportunities for them to practice, students will be better able to determine not only which strategies they are most comfortable using, but which strategies have the greatest impact on reducing their test anxiety.

Positive Self-Talk

Anxiety and negativity are akin to the old chicken and egg situation: Does our anxiety cause us to make negative statements to ourselves, or do our negative self-statements create the anxiety? Let's just say that test anxiety and negative self-talk are inextricably linked—if you find an anxious student, you will probably also find a student who is telling himself or herself that he or she is going to fail. Positive self-talk consists of simple, positive, yet realistic statements that are repeated to oneself in an anxiety-provoking situation. Some examples of positive self-talk include the following:

- ❖ I can do this.
- ❖ I know this material.
- ❖ I have practiced this material.
- ❖ I am intelligent.

The trick to using this strategy is for students to keep the statements simple and to have them practice using them prior to any test-taking situation. You don't want them to have to come up with the statements at the moment they are confronted with the test!

Visualization

There are essentially two types of creative visualization that can be used to help combat test anxiety. Let us call the first type the *Safe Place Method*, which requires students to conjure a mental image of a place, either real or imagined, that is both relaxing and safe. Provide students with the following instructions in order to practice this method:

- ❖ Close your eyes.
- ❖ Calm your breath.
- ❖ Picture your safe place.
- ❖ Look up and down and to the left and to the right of your safe place.
- ❖ Take notice of what you see, smell, and feel.
- ❖ Smile.

Visualization *(cont.)*

The second visualization technique we will call the *Olympic Method*. This method, often used by athletes, requires that individuals imagine what they are trying to achieve, whether it be crossing the finish line first, hitting a home run, or acing a test! Have students practice the following steps:

❖ Close your eyes.

❖ Calm your breath.

❖ Picture yourself confidently taking the test.

❖ Remember another test in which you did well.

❖ Imagine yourself receiving a high test score or grade.

❖ Smile.

Progressive Muscle Relaxation

Anxiety has both a psychological and physiological component. Muscle tension is a common response to test anxiety that can be minimized by using progressive muscle relaxation. This method involves focusing on and then tensing and relaxing large muscle groups in a particular order.

❖ Begin at your toes. Tighten or clench your toes and hold for three to five seconds. Release.

❖ Move upward to your feet, calves, thighs, and so forth. Tighten each muscle group for five seconds, then release.

❖ Once you have moved through your body, take a few deep breaths.

Controlled Breathing

It is a rare person indeed who has never experienced shallow breathing when in an anxiety-filled situation. In fact, shallow, short breaths are a universal indicator of someone who is overwhelmed by anxiety. Practicing controlled breathing is a simple, yet powerful way in which to deal with all kinds of anxiety.

❖ Sit comfortably.

❖ Place your hand on your stomach.

❖ Breathe in gently through your nose for a count of four.

❖ Let your breath expand your belly. Observe your stomach rising.

❖ Breathe out for a count of four.

❖ Observe your stomach flattening.

❖ Repeat.

No doubt you will have noticed that all of the aforementioned techniques have to do with changing what we say, what we see, and what we feel. The mind and the body are woven tightly together like a carpet, and often all one needs to do to "unravel" the pattern of test anxiety woven into the fabric is to pull on one tiny thread. In order for these strategies to be successful, however, students must routinely practice them, especially in non-test taking situations.

Familiarity and proficiency with these methods will empower students and give them the extra tools they need to do their best.

Practice Listening

Most standardized tests that primary students take will be read to them. For this reason, it is imperative that students practice listening. You could say that the listening skills of a first or second grade student are as important in the test-taking scenario as the reading skills are to the older elementary school student.

The purpose of the Practice Listening exercises is to both sharpen students' listening skills and familiarize them with the multiple choice format of testing. Tests at this level contain many choices. The choices are usually pictures, words, or sentences that have circles beneath them for filling in. Students at this age usually do not fill out name grids nor do they have to pace themselves against the clock. The script that you read aloud is their guide to the test and how long they should spend on it.

Answers to several test questions at this age have to do with the context of the pictures. A sample question might be the following:

Which of these children are swimming?

One of the biggest listening challenges first graders face is becoming adept at integrated listening. Integrated listening on a test will require them to listen to a question containing key words like *only*, *between*, *under*, and *unless*, while simultaneously examining possibilities. This is the next step up from simple identification of the correct answer.

Practice Listening

Reproduce, cut, and pass out the animal answer strip below to your students.

Read the script below to students. This exercise will introduce them to the practice of selecting one answer.

Teacher Script

In school, all students take tests so that teachers, parents, and even principals can know more about what you have learned. They can tell partly from the work you do in the classroom and partly from your homework, but a test has a special purpose all its own. A test will check what you know and how you think. A test gives teachers and parents clues about how to help you in school. This is why it's important for you to always try your best when you are taking a test.

Look at the paper strip you were just given. On that strip you will see four animals. Do you see the four animals? What do you notice about them? How are they alike? *(They are all animals. They all have four legs.)*

Which is the only animal for riding? *(the horse)*

When you take a test you get answer choices like this. Your teacher reads a question to you like I just did. You listen to the question. Then you decide which choice is the correct answer. Then you fill in the little circle beneath or next to your answer. If I put a circle on the board, who can show me what to do to the circle on the test? *(Have a student fill in the circle on the board completely, leaving no empty space.)*

That's right. You fill in the circle under the horse.

But what if you fill in a circle and then change your mind? *(You erase it.)* Let's practice erasing. Fill in the circle under an animal other than the horse. *(Pause)* Now pretend that you changed your mind. Erase the wrong one.

It's all right to change your mind. Just make sure that you completely erase the wrong answer and fill in the one you think is correct.

Let's practice taking a test.

Reproduce and pass out page 13 to students.

Read the script below to students. This exercise introduces students to a sample test and gives the students a chance to discuss their answers.

Teacher Script

This is what a test looks like. Pictures are in rows. The questions I will read to you are about the pictures. Choose the picture that answers my question.

Look at the row that has a number 1 beside it. Put your finger on the number 1. *(Make sure students have their fingers on the correct place.)* This is the row of pictures I am going to ask a question about. Listen while I read the question. Which one flies in the wind? Fill in the circle under the picture you choose. *(Pause)* Which circle did you fill in? *(Letter C—the one under the kite.)* That one was easy, wasn't it? Maybe you knew the answer right away.

Look at the row that has the number 2 beside it. Put your finger on the number 2. *(Make sure students have their fingers on the correct place.)* This is the row I am going to ask you a question about. Listen while I read the question. Which is the slowest? *(Pause)* Which circle did you fill in? *(Letter B—the one under the turtle.)* Sometimes you must compare the choices to see which one you think is right.

Look at the row that has the number 3 beside it. Put your finger on the number 3. *(Make sure students have their fingers on the correct place.)* This is the row I am going to ask a question about. How much is 1 + 1? *(Pause)* Which circle did you fill in? *(Letter B—the circle under 2.)* This time you didn't have to compare anything to find the right answer, did you?

Now, put your finger on the number 4. *(Make sure students have their fingers on the correct place.)* Here is the question about this row of pictures. Which animal is the fastest? *(Pause)* Which circle did you fill in? *(Letter D—the one under the horse.)* But wait! These are the same pictures as before. What is the difference? *(You asked for the "fastest" this time.)* Good listening is listening carefully.

Look at the row that has the number 5 beside it. Put your finger on the number 5. Listen while I ask you a question about this row. Which one grows the fastest? *(Pause)* Which circle did you fill in? *(Letter D—the one under the flower.)* All of these things grow, but the flower (the last choice) grows the fastest. That is why you must look at all of the choices before choosing just one.

Now put your finger on the number 6. Listen while I ask you a question. Which is the only girl with a scarf? *(Pause)* Which circle did you fill in? *(Letter C—the third one.)* But there are two children with scarves. Why did you choose the third one? *(Because you said "girl with a scarf.")* It's important to listen to every word in the question.

See the stop sign at the bottom corner? That means it's the end of the test and it's time to stop. Put your pencils down and sit quietly.

Practice Listening

1. Ⓐ Ⓑ Ⓒ Ⓓ

2. Ⓐ Ⓑ Ⓒ Ⓓ

3. 1 2 3 4
   Ⓐ Ⓑ Ⓒ Ⓓ

4. Ⓐ Ⓑ Ⓒ Ⓓ

5. Ⓐ Ⓑ Ⓒ Ⓓ

6. Ⓐ Ⓑ Ⓒ Ⓓ

STOP

Practice Test

Reproduce and pass out page 15 to students.

Read the script below to the students. This exercise gives the students a chance to practice listening by completing a sample test independently.

Teacher Script

Now you are ready to take the practice test. Remember to listen carefully. We will not stop to talk about each question this time. I will ask the question, and you will fill in the circle of your answer. Then I will read the next question. *(Answers appear in the box at the bottom of the page. You can discuss answers with students at the end of the test.)*

Put your finger on the number 1. Has everyone found the number 1? *(Check to make sure students have their fingers beside the correct row.)* Which person is having something to drink?

Put your finger on the number 2. Which picture has only animals in it?

Put your finger on the number 3. Trisha said, "I like small dogs best." Which picture shows Trisha's favorite kind?

Put your finger on the number 4. Gabriel said, "I lost my baseball. Now I can't practice." Which picture shows the ball Gabriel lost?

Put your finger on the number 5. Manny drew a circle on a piece of paper. Then he drew two more shapes. Which picture shows Manny's paper now?

Put your finger on the number 6. Which picture shows two rows of two?

Do you see the stop sign at the bottom of the page? That means stop. Put your pencils down and sit quietly.

Answer Key

1. person drinking something (B)
2. hen, cow, pig (C)
3. smallest dog (D)
4. baseball (A)
5. circle, triangle, and square (B)
6. two rows of two (B)

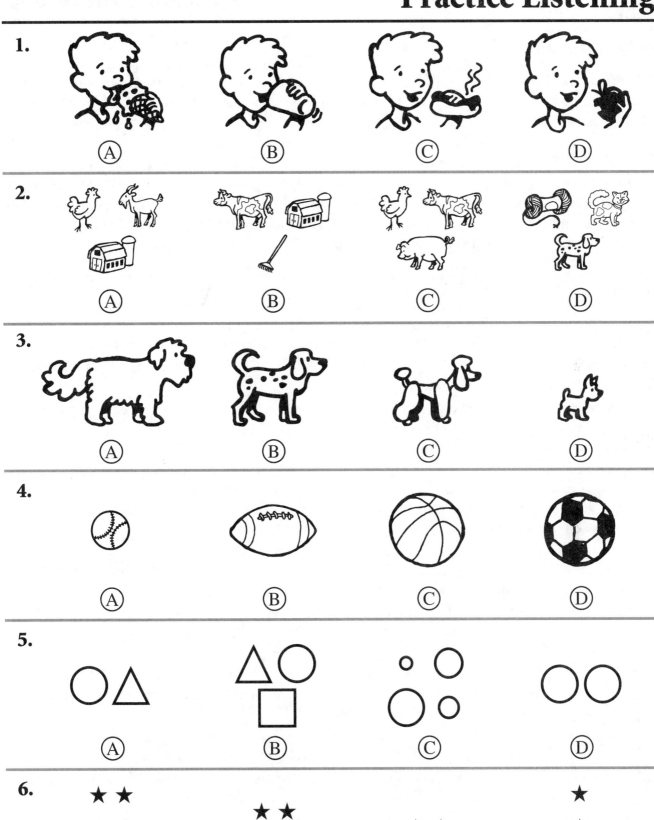

1. Ⓐ Ⓑ Ⓒ Ⓓ

2. Ⓐ Ⓑ Ⓒ Ⓓ

3. Ⓐ Ⓑ Ⓒ Ⓓ

4. Ⓐ Ⓑ Ⓒ Ⓓ

5. Ⓐ Ⓑ Ⓒ Ⓓ

6. Ⓐ Ⓑ Ⓒ Ⓓ **STOP**

Practice Guessing

Sometimes students will not answer a question on a test because they don't know the correct answer. Faced with choices that seem similar, they opt for no answer rather than choose a wrong answer. Furthermore, students will often leave a question unanswered because the material is unfamiliar to them. In this case, students may think they don't know enough to make a choice at all.

Learning the process of elimination teaches students to rely on what they do know. The key to the process is finding information in a question or set of answers that is meaningful to the student. Students may not know what an igloo is, for example, but they can recognize a picture of an ordinary house and a doghouse as not being igloos.

The questions in this section are slightly beyond a second grader's ability level. The purpose is to confront students with a term or a concept or a set of choices that is hard to understand. Emphasize to them that standardized tests are not usually this hard. Explain that they are learning how to get rid of answers that can't be right.

In fact, it is not important that students choose the exact right answer to each question in this section. The goal is to get them to eliminate two obviously wrong choices. On page 18, two right answers will be given for the teacher's script. The better of the two right answers is underlined. It is a good idea to go over the questions and answers in the tests right away to reinforce student's understanding of how the process of elimination works.

Reproduce and pass out page 17 to students.

Read the script below to students. The exercise encourages students to make good guesses at the correct answers by using the process of elimination.

Teacher Script

Sometimes you have to guess on a test. You may think, "I don't know the answer to this question," or "I'm not sure of the answer." But you should always answer every question. You might have to guess. We are going to learn how to make good guesses.

We are now going to play a guessing game called "Which animal is the most popular at the zoo?" This is how we play. I will think of an animal. Then I will give you clues. You will listen and cross out the animal that can't be the one that I am thinking of.

Put your finger on number 1. In this row there is a turtle, a lion, a giraffe, an elephant, and an ostrich. The animal I am thinking of has four feet. Which animal can't be the one I am thinking of? *(the ostrich)* Cross it out.

Put your finger on number 2. Now the ostrich is gone, and there is a turtle, a lion, a giraffe, and an elephant. The animal I am thinking of has a short neck. Which animal can't be the one I am thinking of? *(the giraffe)* Cross it out. There are three animals left.

Put your finger on number 3. Here are the three animals that are left. The animal I am thinking of does not have a shell. Which animal can't be the one I am thinking of? *(the turtle)* Cross it out.

Put your finger on number 4. There are two animals left. The animal I am thinking of has fur. Which animal can't be the one that I am thinking of? *(the elephant)* Cross it out.

So which animal is the most popular at the zoo? *(the lion)*

How did you figure out the animal I was thinking of? *(listened for clues; crossed out some animals)* The more wrong answers you can get rid of, the easier it is to guess the right answer. Remember to answer every question on a test. Sometimes you will have to guess. Nobody can know everything there is to know! But first, get rid of the answers you know are not right. This will make you a good guesser.

Practice Guessing

Which animal is the most popular at the zoo?

1.

○　　　○　　　○　　　○　　　○

2.

○　　　○　　　○　　　○

3.

○　　　○　　　○

4.

○　　　○

Practice Guessing

Reproduce and pass out page 19 to students.

Read the script below to students. This exercise introduces them to a sample test and gives the students a chance to discuss their answers.

Teacher Script

Now we have rows of four pictures. We are going to practice getting rid of answers that can't be correct. This time the questions are hard. These questions are harder than the ones you will see on a real test. But I want you to get rid of two answers that can't be right.

Put your finger on number 1. An accountant is someone who works inside an office. Which one is a picture of an accountant? Look at the four pictures. Remember what you learned about guessing. Get rid of two answers that can't be right. This time, don't cross them out. Guess which answer is right. Fill in the circle for your guess. *(Pause) (doctor or* _accountant_*)* Why did you get rid of the other two? *(They show people working outside and an accountant works inside in an office.)* Remember to get rid of answers that can't be right and then guess.

Put your finger on number 2. This is the row I am going to ask you a question about. A whisk is very useful for making a cake. Which one is a whisk? Remember to get rid of the two that can't be right. *(Pause)* Now guess and fill in the circle of your guess. Which one did you choose? *(the wire* _whisk_ *or the spatula)* Why did you get rid of the other two? *(A screwdriver and a ball are not useful for making a cake.)* You are making good guesses now.

Put your finger on number 3. This row has four numbers in it. Listen while I ask the question. *(Pause)* André is seven years old. His sister Tasha is two times older than André. How old is André's sister? Get rid of the two answers that can't be right. Fill in the circle of your guess. *(Pause)* Which number did you guess? *(12 or* _14_*)* Why did you get of the other two? *(Because 5 and 2 are less than 7, and Tasha is older than André.)*

Put your finger on number 4. This question is about a house. Mr. Anderson's roof has a gable that's 14 feet high. Which picture shows Mr. Anderson's gable? *(Pause)* Guess and fill in the circle. Which one did you guess? *(the chimney or the* _gable_*)* Why did you get rid of the other two? *(You couldn't see a roof at all.)*

Put your finger on number 5. This is the last question. It's about shapes. Which picture shows a right triangle? *(Pause)* Get rid of two. Make your guess and fill in the circle. *(Pause)* Which one did you choose? *(the scalene or the* _right triangle_*)* Why didn't you choose the other two? *(They are not triangles.)* Learning to be a good guesser is learning to get rid of answers than can't be right.

1.

Ⓐ   Ⓑ   Ⓒ   Ⓓ

2.

Ⓐ   Ⓑ   Ⓒ   Ⓓ

3.

14   12   5   2

Ⓐ   Ⓑ   Ⓒ   Ⓓ

4.

Ⓐ   Ⓑ   Ⓒ   Ⓓ

5.

Ⓐ   Ⓑ   Ⓒ   Ⓓ

Reproduce and pass out page 21 to students.

Read the script below to students. This sample test will help them practice guessing independently.

Teacher Script

Now that we have done some questions together and talked about them, it's time for you to try some on your own. I will ask a question about the pictures in each row. You will get rid of two answers. Then you will make a good guess and fill in the circle under it. We will not talk about your guesses until the end. You must listen quietly to the questions.

Put your finger on number 1. I am going to ask you a question about this row of pictures. Listen to the question. A long time ago, people wrote with quill pens. Which picture shows a quill pen? Fill in the circle under the correct answer.

Put your finger on number 2. Here is the next question. Jessica said, "Look! That fish sees its reflection in the mirror." Which picture shows a fish looking at its reflection? Make a good guess and fill in the correct circle.

Put your finger on number 3. Here is the question. Mr. Webb's umbrella protected him from the inclement weather. Which picture shows Mr. Webb protected by his umbrella? Fill in the correct circle.

Put your finger on number 4. Here is the question. Mother said, "When you start to set the table, please make the plates symmetrical. That looks neater." Which picture shows the table set the way Mother wants it? Fill in the correct circle.

Put your finger on number 5. Here is the question. Crustaceans are sea animals whose bodies are covered by hard shells. Which picture shows a crustacean? Fill in the correct circle.

Put your finger on number 6. Here is the question. Which picture shows three parallel lines? Fill in the correct circle.

Do you see the stop sign at the bottom of the page? That means stop. I'll know you are finished when your pencil is down and you are sitting quietly.

Answer Key

1. D
2. B
3. C
4. B
5. C
6. B

1. Ⓐ Ⓑ Ⓒ Ⓓ

2. Ⓐ Ⓑ Ⓒ Ⓓ

3. Ⓐ Ⓑ Ⓒ Ⓓ

4. Ⓐ Ⓑ Ⓒ Ⓓ

5. Ⓐ Ⓑ Ⓒ Ⓓ

6. Ⓐ Ⓑ Ⓒ Ⓓ

STOP

Sentences

Reproduce and pass out page 23 to students.

Teacher Script

In this test, we are going to practice finding complete sentences. You will have to read three groups of words. Then, you will have to decide which group of words is a complete sentence. Once you have decided, you will fill in the circle next to the correct answer. First, let's do one together.

Put your finger on the sample. Read each group of words to yourself. Now, which one is the complete sentence? Yes, B. *The boy took a walk*. This is the complete sentence. Fill in the letter B answer circle. Good job. Now let's begin.

Put your finger on number 1. Read each group of words to yourself. Find the complete sentence. Now, fill in the correct answer circle.

Put your finger on number 2. Read each group of words to yourself. Find the complete sentence. Now, fill in the correct answer circle.

Put your finger on number 3. Read each group of words to yourself. Find the complete sentence. Now, fill in the correct answer circle.

Put your finger on number 4. Read each group of words to yourself. Find the complete sentence. Now, fill in the correct answer circle.

Put your finger on number 5. Read each group of words to yourself. Find the complete sentence. Now, fill in the correct answer circle.

Put your finger on number 6. Read each group of words to yourself. Find the complete sentence. Now, fill in the correct answer circle.

Put your finger on number 7. Read each group of words to yourself. Find the complete sentence. Now, fill in the correct answer circle.

Put your finger on number 8. Read each group of words to yourself. Find the complete sentence. Now, fill in the correct answer circle.

Now we stop.

Answer Key

1. A
2. C
3. B
4. A
5. C
6. A
7. B
8. C

Sentences

Sample: (A) took a walk.

(B) The boy took a walk.

(C) The boy.

---

1. (A) I like to play basketball.

   (B) to play basketball.

   (C) I like.

2. (A) on Monday.

   (B) We have.

   (C) We have gym class on Mondays.

3. (A) to the movies last night.

   (B) We went to the movies last night.

   (C) We went to the.

4. (A) Keisha told a funny joke.

   (B) a funny joke.

   (C) Keisha told.

5. (A) Ran all the way home.

   (B) all the way home.

   (C) It started to rain so I ran all the way home.

6. (A) Yesterday, I went to the zoo.

   (B) to the zoo.

   (C) Went to the zoo.

7. (A) Won the race!

   (B) John won the race!

   (C) the race!

8. (A) built a snowman.

   (B) My sister built.

   (C) My sister and I built a snowman.

STOP

Sight Words

Reproduce and pass out page 25 to students.

Teacher Script

Now we are going to identify some sight words. I will give you a direction for each group of words, and you will fill in the answer. I will not stop to discuss the directions, but I will go slowly enough for you to answer each one. When you are finished, put your pencil down and sit quietly. Let's begin.

Put your finger on number 1. Find the word that says *always*. (Repeat direction.) Fill in the correct answer circle.

Put your finger on number 2. Find the word that says *green*. (Repeat direction.) Fill in the correct answer circle.

Put your finger on number 3. Find the word that says *pull*. (Repeat direction.) Fill in the correct answer circle.

Put your finger on number 4. Find the word that says *why*. (Repeat direction.) Fill in the correct answer circle.

Put your finger on number 5. Find the word that says *write*. (Repeat direction.) Fill in the correct answer circle.

Put your finger on number 6. Find the word that says *before*. (Repeat direction.) Fill in the correct answer circle.

Put your finger on number 7. Find the word that says *made*. (Repeat direction.) Fill in the correct answer circle.

Put your finger on number 8. Find the word that says *wish*. (Repeat direction.) Fill in the correct answer circle.

Put your finger on number 9. Find the word that says *sing*. (Repeat direction.) Fill in the correct answer circle.

Put your finger on number 10. Find the word that says *these*. (Repeat direction.) Fill in the correct answer circle.

Now we stop.

Answer Key

1. A	**6.** B
2. C	**7.** C
3. A	**8.** C
4. C	**9.** B
5. A	**10.** C

Sight Words

1. (A) always
    (B) found
    (C) around

2. (A) use
    (B) first
    (C) green

3. (A) pull
    (B) pretty
    (C) put

4. (A) call
    (B) cold
    (C) why

5. (A) write
    (B) gave
    (C) read

6. (A) because
    (B) before
    (C) brown

7. (A) many
    (B) may
    (C) made

8. (A) work
    (B) where
    (C) wish

9. (A) stop
    (B) sing
    (C) now

10. (A) thank
    (B) that
    (C) these

STOP

Types of Sentences

Reproduce and pass out page 27 to students.

Teacher Script

In this test, we are going to practice identifying different types of sentences. I will ask you a question about each group of phrases, and you will fill in the answer. I will not stop to discuss the questions, but I will go slowly enough for you to answer each one. When you are finished, put your pencil down and sit quietly. Let's do one together first.

Put your finger on the sample. Which sentence is a command? (Repeat question.) Read each sentence. Which one did you choose? That's right. It's C. *Please pick up the trash.* Fill in the letter C answer circle. Now we will begin.

Put your finger on number 1. Which sentence is a question? (Repeat question.) Read each sentence. Fill in the correct answer circle.

Put your finger on number 2. Which sentence is a statement? (Repeat question.) Read each sentence. Fill in the correct answer circle.

Put your finger on number 3. Which sentence is a command? (Repeat question.) Read each sentence. Fill in the correct answer circle.

Put your finger on number 4. Which sentence is an exclamation? (Repeat question.) Read each sentence. Fill in the correct answer circle.

Put your finger on number 5. Which sentence is an exclamation? (Repeat question.) Read each sentence. Fill in the correct answer circle.

Put your finger on number 6. Which sentence is a command? (Repeat question.) Read each sentence. Fill in the correct answer circle.

Put your finger on number 7. Which sentence is a statement? (Repeat question.) Read each sentence. Fill in the correct answer circle.

Put your finger on number 8. Which sentence is a question? (Repeat question.) Read each sentence. Fill in the correct answer circle.

Put your finger on number 9. Which sentence is a command? (Repeat question.) Read each sentence. Fill in the correct answer circle.

Put your finger on number 10. Which sentence is a statement? (Repeat question.) Read each sentence. Fill in the correct answer circle.

Now we stop. I'll know you're finished when your pencil is down and you're sitting quietly.

Answer Key

1. C	6. B
2. A	7. B
3. C	8. A
4. B	9. B
5. A	10. A

Types of Sentences

1. Ⓐ It is warm outside.
   Ⓑ Stop talking!
   Ⓒ What is your favorite movie?

2. Ⓐ My father works in a bank.
   Ⓑ May I borrow a pencil?
   Ⓒ My head hurts!

3. Ⓐ When is your birthday?
   Ⓑ We live on planet Earth.
   Ⓒ Please clean your room.

4. Ⓐ I have homework every night.
   Ⓑ I won first place!
   Ⓒ What time is it?

5. Ⓐ I'm going to miss the bus!
   Ⓑ Please pass the corn.
   Ⓒ I am a good swimmer.

6. Ⓐ Can I have an ice cream?
   Ⓑ Move your bike into the yard.
   Ⓒ We walk to school.

7. Ⓐ Why is it so cloudy?
   Ⓑ We ran five miles this week.
   Ⓒ I lost my ring!

8. Ⓐ Who is on the phone?
   Ⓑ My friend lives next door to me.
   Ⓒ I go to bed at 8:30.

9. Ⓐ Where are my socks?
   Ⓑ Please go to the store.
   Ⓒ I like to sing.

10. Ⓐ Green is my favorite color.
    Ⓑ How many pennies did you count?
    Ⓒ Ouch, my finger hurts!

End Marks

Reproduce and pass out page 29 to students.

Teacher Script

In this test, we are going to practice identifying different types of punctuation. I will ask you a question about each sentence, and you will fill in the answer. I will not stop to discuss the questions, but I will go slowly enough for you to answer each one. When you are finished, put your pencil down and sit quietly. Let's do one together first.

Put your finger on the sample. Read the sentence. Now decide which end mark the sentence needs. (Repeat question.) Which one did you choose? That's right. It's A because this sentence is a question, so it needs a question mark. Fill in the correct answer circle. Now we will begin.

Put your finger on number 1. Read the sentence. Which end mark does this sentence need? (Repeat question.) Fill in the correct answer circle.

Put your finger on number 2. Read the sentence. Which end mark does this sentence need? (Repeat question.) Fill in the correct answer circle.

Put your finger on number 3. Read the sentence. Which end mark does this sentence need? (Repeat question.) Fill in the correct answer circle.

Put your finger on number 4. Read the sentence. Which end mark does this sentence need? (Repeat question.) Fill in the correct answer circle.

Put your finger on number 5. Read the sentence. Which end mark does this sentence need? (Repeat question.) Fill in the correct answer circle.

Put your finger on number 6. Read the sentence. Which end mark does this sentence need? (Repeat question.) Fill in the correct answer circle.

Put your finger on number 7. Read the sentence. Which end mark does this sentence need? (Repeat question.) Fill in the correct answer circle.

Put your finger on number 8. Read the sentence. Which end mark does this sentence need? (Repeat question.) Fill in the correct answer circle.

Put your finger on number 9. Read the sentence. Which end mark does this sentence need? (Repeat question.) Fill in the correct answer circle.

Put your finger on number 10. Read the sentence. Which end mark does this sentence need? (Repeat question.) Fill in the correct answer circle.

Now we stop.

Answer Key

1. B	6. C
2. C	7. B
3. B	8. B
4. B	9. B
5. A	10. C

End Marks

Sample: How do you do that card trick
- Ⓐ question mark (?)
- Ⓑ period (.)
- Ⓒ exclamation point (!)

---

1. I baked some cookies with my friend
- Ⓐ question mark (?)
- Ⓑ period (.)
- Ⓒ exclamation point (!)

2. Stop before you get hurt
- Ⓐ question mark (?)
- Ⓑ period (.)
- Ⓒ exclamation point (!)

3. I like that song
- Ⓐ question mark (?)
- Ⓑ period (.)
- Ⓒ exclamation point (!)

4. Please put your shoes away
- Ⓐ question mark (?)
- Ⓑ period (.)
- Ⓒ exclamation point (!)

5. May I have a piece of cake
- Ⓐ question mark (?)
- Ⓑ period (.)
- Ⓒ exclamation point (!)

6. The movie was so scary
- Ⓐ question mark (?)
- Ⓑ period (.)
- Ⓒ exclamation point (!)

7. Kwanzaa is celebrated in December
- Ⓐ question mark (?)
- Ⓑ period (.)
- Ⓒ exclamation point (!)

8. It is very sunny today
- Ⓐ question mark (?)
- Ⓑ period (.)
- Ⓒ exclamation point (!)

9. Put the book on the shelf
- Ⓐ question mark (?)
- Ⓑ period (.)
- Ⓒ exclamation point (!)

10. Oh no, I broke the vase
- Ⓐ question mark (?)
- Ⓑ period (.)
- Ⓒ exclamation point (!)

Short and Long Vowels

Reproduce and pass out page 31 to students.

Teacher Script

In this test, we are going to practice identifying vowel sounds. I will give you a direction for each row, and you will fill in the answer. I will not stop to discuss the directions, but I will go slowly enough for you to answer each one. When you are finished, put your pencil down and sit quietly.

Put your finger on number 1. Read the words silently. Find the word that has the short vowel sound. (Repeat direction.) Fill in the correct answer circle.

Put your finger on number 2. Read the words silently. Find the word that has the long vowel sound. (Repeat direction.) Fill in the correct answer circle.

Put your finger on number 3. Read the words silently. Find the word that has the long vowel sound. (Repeat direction.) Fill in the correct answer circle.

Put your finger on number 4. Read the words silently. Find the word that has the short vowel sound. (Repeat direction.) Fill in the correct answer circle.

Put your finger on number 5. Read the words silently. Find the word that has the long vowel sound. (Repeat direction.) Fill in the correct answer circle.

Put your finger on number 6. Read the words silently. Find the word that has the short vowel sound. (Repeat direction.) Fill in the correct answer circle.

Put your finger on number 7. Read the words silently. Find the word that has the short vowel sound. (Repeat direction.) Fill in the correct answer circle.

Put your finger on number 8. Read the words silently. Find the word that has the long vowel sound. (Repeat direction.) Fill in the correct answer circle.

Put your finger on number 9. Read the words silently. Find the word that has the short vowel sound. (Repeat direction.) Fill in the correct answer circle.

Put your finger on number 10. Read the words silently. Find the word that has the long vowel sound. (Repeat direction.) Fill in the correct answer circle.

Now we stop.

Answer Key	
1. A	**6.** D
2. B	**7.** C
3. A	**8.** B
4. C	**9.** D
5. B	**10.** A

Short and Long Vowels

1. pig Ⓐ   play Ⓑ   pie Ⓒ   over Ⓓ

2. egg Ⓐ   even Ⓑ   boy Ⓒ   camp Ⓓ

3. open Ⓐ   can Ⓑ   cat Ⓒ   pin Ⓓ

4. lake Ⓐ   kite Ⓑ   drop Ⓒ   grape Ⓓ

5. skip Ⓐ   skate Ⓑ   mix Ⓒ   bag Ⓓ

6. goat Ⓐ   take Ⓑ   mice Ⓒ   pen Ⓓ

7. nine Ⓐ   plate Ⓑ   rug Ⓒ   free Ⓓ

8. get Ⓐ   gave Ⓑ   win Ⓒ   mitten Ⓓ

9. show Ⓐ   seed Ⓑ   stripe Ⓒ   sip Ⓓ

10. cube Ⓐ   bat Ⓑ   hot Ⓒ   thick Ⓓ

STOP

Subjects and Predicates

Reproduce and pass out page 33 to students.

Teacher Script

In this test, we are going to practice identifying subjects and predicates. I will ask you a question about each sentence, and you will fill in the answer. I will not stop to discuss the questions, but I will go slowly enough for you to finish each one. When you are finished, put your pencil down and sit quietly. Let's do one together first.

Put your finger on the sample. Read the sentence. Which part of the sentence is underlined? That's right. The *I* is underlined. Now ask yourself, is the underlined part of the sentence the subject or the predicate? That's correct. It is the subject. It tells who or what the sentence is about. Fill in the letter A answer circle. Now we will begin.

Put your finger on number 1. Read the sentence silently. Is the underlined part of the sentence the subject or the predicate? (Repeat question.) Fill in the correct answer circle.

Put your finger on number 2. Read the sentence silently. Is the underlined part of the sentence the subject or the predicate? (Repeat question.) Fill in the correct answer circle.

Put your finger on number 3. Read the sentence silently. Is the underlined part of the sentence the subject or the predicate? (Repeat question.) Fill in the correct answer circle.

Put your finger on number 4. Read the sentence silently. Is the underlined part of the sentence the subject or the predicate? (Repeat question.) Fill in the correct answer circle.

Put your finger on number 5. Read the sentence silently. Is the underlined part of the sentence the subject or the predicate? (Repeat question.) Fill in the correct answer circle.

Put your finger on number 6. Read the sentence silently. Is the underlined part of the sentence the subject or the predicate? (Repeat question.) Fill in the correct answer circle.

Put your finger on number 7. Read the sentence silently. Is the underlined part of the sentence the subject or the predicate? (Repeat question.) Fill in the correct answer circle.

Put your finger on number 8. Read the sentence silently. Is the underlined part of the sentence the subject or the predicate? (Repeat question.) Fill in the correct answer circle.

Put your finger on number 9. Read the sentence silently. Is the underlined part of the sentence the subject or the predicate? (Repeat question.) Fill in the correct answer circle.

Put your finger on number 10. Read the sentence silently. Is the underlined part of the sentence the subject or the predicate? (Repeat question.) Fill in the correct answer circle.

Now we stop.

Answer Key

1.	B	6.	B
2.	B	7.	B
3.	A	8.	A
4.	A	9.	A
5.	A	10.	B

Subjects and Predicates

Sample: I went to the mall last night.
Ⓐ   subject
Ⓑ   predicate

---

1. The dog is black with white spots.
   Ⓐ subject
   Ⓑ predicate

2. Yesterday, I had chicken for supper.
   Ⓐ subject
   Ⓑ predicate

3. My friend, Jamal and I went to play baseball.
   Ⓐ subject
   Ⓑ predicate

4. She wants to be a teacher when she grows up.
   Ⓐ subject
   Ⓑ predicate

5. Sam, Jane, and Greg all have colds.
   Ⓐ subject
   Ⓑ predicate

6. Tony ran the fastest and won the race.
   Ⓐ subject
   Ⓑ predicate

7. Mrs. Jackson wrote the math homework on the board.
   Ⓐ subject
   Ⓑ predicate

8. The play was about Johnny Appleseed.
   Ⓐ subject
   Ⓑ predicate

9. The colors of the flag are red, white, and blue.
   Ⓐ subject
   Ⓑ predicate

10. The music was really good.
    Ⓐ subject
    Ⓑ predicate

STOP

Sentence Combining

Reproduce and pass out page 35 to students.

Teacher Script

In this test, we are going to practice combining sentences. I will give you a direction for each set of sentences, and you will fill in the answer. I will not stop to discuss the directions, but I will go slowly enough for you to finish each one. When you are finished, put your pencil down and sit quietly. First, let's do one together.

Put your finger on the sample. There are two sentences. Read each sentence silently. Now you see three choices. You need to find the choice that best combines both sentences. Which one did you choose? Yes, C is correct, because *It is hot and sunny* best combines both sentences. Fill in the correct answer circle. Now let's begin.

Put your finger on number 1. There are two sentences. Read each sentence silently. Find the choice that best combines both sentences. Fill in the correct answer circle.

Put your finger on number 2. There are two sentences. Read each sentence silently. Find the choice that best combines both sentences. Fill in the correct answer circle.

Put your finger on number 3. There are two sentences. Read each sentence silently. Find the choice that best combines both sentences. Fill in the correct answer circle.

Put your finger on number 4. There are two sentences. Read each sentence silently. Find the choice that best combines both sentences. Fill in the correct answer circle.

Put your finger on number 5. There are two sentences. Read each sentence silently. Find the choice that best combines both sentences. Fill in the correct answer circle.

Put your finger on number 6. There are two sentences. Read each sentence silently. Find the choice that best combines both sentences. Fill in the correct answer circle.

Put your finger on number 7. There are two sentences. Read each sentence silently. Find the choice that best combines both sentences. Fill in the correct answer circle.

Put your finger on number 8. There are two sentences. Read each sentence silently. Find the choice that best combines both sentences. Fill in the correct answer circle.

Now we stop.

Answer Key

1. A	**5.** A
2. B	**6.** C
3. B	**7.** B
4. C	**8.** A

Sentence Combining

> **Sample:** It is hot. It is sunny.
> - (A) Hot and sunny it is.
> - (B) Hot and sunny is it.
> - (C) It is hot and sunny.

1. I like spaghetti. I like meatballs.
- Ⓐ I like spaghetti and meatballs.
- (B) Spaghetti and meatballs I like.
- (C) Meatballs and spaghetti I like.

2. I want new shoes. My sister wants new shoes.
- (A) Want new shoes both me and my sister.
- Ⓑ My sister and I want new shoes.
- (C) I want new shoes and my sister wants new shoes.

3. I studied my spelling. I studied my math.
- (A) Spelling and math I studied.
- Ⓑ I studied my spelling and math.
- (C) I studied math and I also studied spelling.

4. The cat is black. The cat is white.
- (A) Black and white the cat is.
- (B) The cat is black and the cat is white.
- Ⓒ The cat is black and white.

5. I wore green pants. I went to the party.
- Ⓐ I wore green pants to the party.
- (B) I went to the party and wore green pants.
- (C) To the party I went and wore green pants.

6. I took out the trash. I put my bike away.
- (A) I took out the trash and I put my bike away.
- (B) The trash I took out and put my bike away.
- Ⓒ I took out the trash and put my bike away.

7. My best friend is Calvin. He lives next door to me.
- (A) Next door to me my best friend Calvin lives.
- Ⓑ My best friend, Calvin, lives next door to me.
- (C) Lives next door to me, Calvin, my best friend.

8. My dog likes to run. My dog likes to jump.
- Ⓐ My dog likes to run and jump.
- (B) Run and jump my dog likes.
- (C) My dog likes to run and my dog likes to jump.

STOP

Reproduce and pass out page 37 to students.

Teacher Script

In this test, we are going to practice identifying the sounds at the beginning of words. I will ask you a question about each row, and you will fill in the answer. I will not stop to discuss the questions, but I will go slowly enough for you to finish each one. When you are finished, put your pencil down and sit quietly.

Put your finger on number 1. Look at the first picture. Now look at the three pictures next to it. Which one has the same beginning sound as the first picture? Fill in the correct answer circle.

Put your finger on number 2. Look at the first picture. Now look at the three pictures next to it. Which one has the same beginning sound as the first picture? Fill in the correct answer circle.

Put your finger on number 3. Look at the first picture. Now look at the three pictures next to it. Which one has the same beginning sound as the first picture? Fill in the correct answer circle.

Put your finger on number 4. Look at the first picture. Now look at the three pictures next to it. Which one has the same beginning sound as the first picture? Fill in the correct answer circle.

Put your finger on number 5. Look at the first picture. Now look at the three pictures next to it. Which one has the same beginning sound as the first picture? Fill in the correct answer circle.

Put your finger on number 6. Look at the first picture. Now look at the three pictures next to it. Which one has the same beginning sound as the first picture? Fill in the correct answer circle.

Put your finger on number 7. Look at the first picture. Now look at the three pictures next to it. Which one has the same beginning sound as the first picture? Fill in the correct answer circle.

Put your finger on number 8. Look at the first picture. Now look at the three pictures next to it. Which one has the same beginning sound as the first picture? Fill in the correct answer circle.

Put your finger on number 9. Look at the first picture. Now look at the three pictures next to it. Which one has the same beginning sound as the first picture? Fill in the correct answer circle.

Put your finger on number 10. Look at the first picture. Now look at the three pictures next to it. Which one has the same beginning sound as the first picture? Fill in the correct answer circle.

Now we stop.

Answer Key

1. C	**6.** C
2. B	**7.** A
3. A	**8.** B
4. C	**9.** B
5. B	**10.** C

Beginning Sounds

1. A   B   C

2. A   B   C

3. A   B   C

4. A   B   C

5. A   B   C

6. A   B   C

7. A   B   C

8. A   B   C

9. A   B   C

10. A   B   C

STOP

Ending Sounds

Reproduce and pass out page 39 to students.

Teacher Script

In this test, we are going to practice identifying the sounds at the end of words. I will ask you a question about each row, and you will fill in the answer. I will not stop to discuss the questions, but I will go slowly enough for you to finish each one. When you are finished, put your pencil down and sit quietly.

Put your finger on number 1. Look at the first picture. Now look at the three pictures next to it. Which one has the same ending sound as the first picture? Fill in the correct answer circle.

Put your finger on number 2. Look at the first picture. Now look at the three pictures next to it. Which one has the same ending sound as the first picture? Fill in the correct answer circle.

Put your finger on number 3. Look at the first picture. Now look at the three pictures next to it. Which one has the same ending sound as the first picture? Fill in the correct answer circle.

Put your finger on number 4. Look at the first picture. Now look at the three pictures next to it. Which one has the same ending sound as the first picture? Fill in the correct answer circle.

Put your finger on number 5. Look at the first picture. Now look at the three pictures next to it. Which one has the same ending sound as the first picture? Fill in the correct answer circle.

Put your finger on number 6. Look at the first picture. Now look at the three pictures next to it. Which one has the same ending sound as the first picture? Fill in the correct answer circle.

Put your finger on number 7. Look at the first picture. Now look at the three pictures next to it. Which one has the same ending sound as the first picture? Fill in the correct answer circle.

Put your finger on number 8. Look at the first picture. Now look at the three pictures next to it. Which one has the same ending sound as the first picture? Fill in the correct answer circle.

Put your finger on number 9. Look at the first picture. Now look at the three pictures next to it. Which one has the same ending sound as the first picture? Fill in the correct answer circle.

Put your finger on number 10. Look at the first picture. Now look at the three pictures next to it. Which one has the same ending sound as the first picture? Fill in the correct answer circle.

Now we stop.

Answer Key	
1. A	6. B
2. B	7. A
3. C	8. B
4. B	9. C
5. A	10. B

Ending Sounds

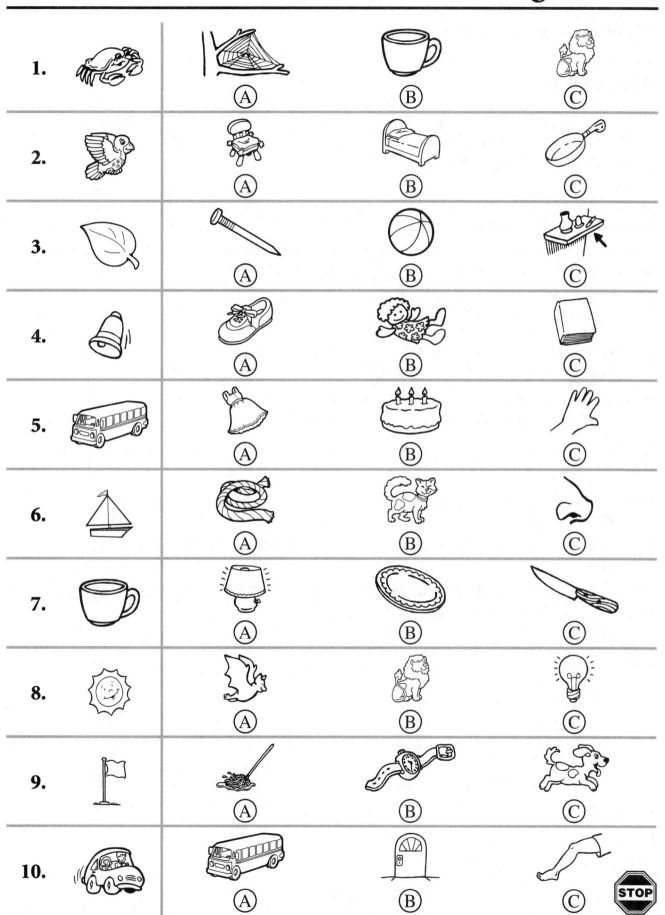

1. A   B   C

2. A   B   C

3. A   B   C

4. A   B   C

5. A   B   C

6. A   B   C

7. A   B   C

8. A   B   C

9. A   B   C

10. A   B   C

STOP

Reproduce and pass out page 41 to students.

Teacher Script

In this test, we are going to practice identifying nouns, proper nouns, verbs, and adjectives. I will ask you a question about each sentence, and you will fill in the answer. I will not stop to discuss the questions, but I will go slowly enough for you to finish each one. When you are finished, put your pencil down and sit quietly. First, let's do one together.

Put your finger on the sample. Read the sentence silently. You will notice that one or more of the words in the sentence are underlined. Which part of speech is the underlined word? Is it a noun, a verb, or an adjective? Right, *fast* is an adjective. Fill in the correct answer circle. Now let's begin.

Put your finger on number 1. Read the sentence silently. Which part of speech is the underlined word? Fill in the correct answer circle.

Put your finger on number 2. Read the sentence silently. Which part of speech is the underlined word? Fill in the correct answer circle.

Put your finger on number 3. Read the sentence silently. Which part of speech is the underlined word? Fill in the correct answer circle.

Put your finger on number 4. Read the sentence silently. Which part of speech is the underlined word? Fill in the correct answer circle.

Put your finger on number 5. Read the sentence silently. Which part of speech is the underlined word? Fill in the correct answer circle.

Put your finger on number 6. Read the sentence silently. Which part of speech are the underlined words? Fill in the correct answer circle.

Put your finger on number 7. Read the sentence silently. Which part of speech is the underlined word? Fill in the correct answer circle.

Put your finger on number 8. Read the sentence silently. Which part of speech is the underlined word? Fill in the correct answer circle.

Put your finger on number 9. Read the sentence silently. Which part of speech is the underlined word? Fill in the correct answer circle.

Put your finger on number 10. Read the sentence silently. Which part of speech is the underlined word? Fill in the correct answer circle.

Now we stop.

Answer Key

1.	B	6.	A
2.	A	7.	B
3.	C	8.	C
4.	A	9.	C
5.	B	10.	B

Parts of Speech

Sample: John is a <u>fast</u> runner.
- (A) noun
- (B) verb
- (C) adjective

---

1. My little brother <u>giggles</u> all the time.
   - (A) noun
   - (B) verb
   - (C) adjective

2. How many <u>books</u> do you have?
   - (A) noun
   - (B) verb
   - (C) adjective

3. I am <u>seven</u> years old.
   - (A) noun
   - (B) verb
   - (C) adjective

4. My teacher's name is <u>Ms. Wells</u>.
   - (A) proper noun
   - (B) verb
   - (C) adjective

5. The flowers <u>are</u> pink and yellow.
   - (A) noun
   - (B) verb
   - (C) adjective

6. <u>Juan</u> and <u>Miguel</u> are brothers.
   - (A) proper nouns
   - (B) verbs
   - (C) adjectives

7. Anton is <u>singing</u> in the chorus.
   - (A) noun
   - (B) verb
   - (C) adjective

8. Our school is in a <u>new</u> building.
   - (A) noun
   - (B) verb
   - (C) adjective

9. Katherine came in <u>first</u> in the race.
   - (A) noun
   - (B) verb
   - (C) adjective

10. My cat <u>is</u> called Thomas.
    - (A) noun
    - (B) verb
    - (C) adjective

STOP

Reproduce and pass out page 43 to students.

Teacher Script

In this test, we are going to practice identifying consonant blends. I will give you a direction for each picture, and you will fill in the answer. I will not stop to discuss the directions, but I will go slowly enough for you to finish each one. When you are finished, put your pencil down and sit quietly.

Put your finger on the sample. Look at the picture. What is this a picture of? That's right. It's a flag. Now look at the three choices. You have to find the blend that begins the word *flag*. Which one did you choose? Right again. It's B, because the blend *fl* begins the word *flag*. Fill in the correct answer circle. Now let's begin.

Put your finger on number 1. Look at the picture. Find the blend that this picture begins with. Fill in the correct answer circle.

Put your finger on number 2. Look at the picture. Find the blend that this picture begins with. Fill in the correct answer circle.

Put your finger on number 3. Look at the picture. Find the blend that this picture begins with. Fill in the correct answer circle.

Put your finger on number 4. Look at the picture. Find the blend that this picture begins with. Fill in the correct answer circle.

Put your finger on number 5. Look at the picture. Find the blend that this picture begins with. Fill in the correct answer circle.

Put your finger on number 6. Look at the picture. Find the blend that this picture begins with. Fill in the correct answer circle.

Put your finger on number 7. Look at the picture. Find the blend that this picture begins with. Fill in the correct answer circle.

Put your finger on number 8. Look at the picture. Find the blend that this picture begins with. Fill in the correct answer circle.

Put your finger on number 9. Look at the picture. Find the blend that this picture begins with. Fill in the correct answer circle.

Put your finger on number 10. Look at the picture. Find the blend that this picture begins with. Fill in the correct answer circle.

Now we stop.

Answer Key

1. B	6. B
2. A	7. B
3. C	8. B
4. C	9. B
5. B	10. C

Letter Blends

Sample:
- (A) pl
- (B) fl
- (C) sn

1.
- (A) br
- (B) sl
- (C) sw

2.
- (A) dr
- (B) st
- (C) sk

3.
- (A) br
- (B) ch
- (C) dr

4.
- (A) fl
- (B) gl
- (C) fr

5.
- (A) cr
- (B) cl
- (C) tr

6.
- (A) pr
- (B) tr
- (C) st

7.
- (A) st
- (B) sn
- (C) sw

8.
- (A) fr
- (B) sw
- (C) gl

9.
- (A) cr
- (B) cl
- (C) sk

10.
- (A) st
- (B) sw
- (C) sp

Plural Nouns

Reproduce and pass out page 45 to students.

Teacher Script

In this test, we are going to practice identifying plural nouns. I will give you a direction for each group of words, and you will fill in the answer. I will not stop to discuss the directions, but I will go slowly enough for you to finish each one. When you are finished, put your pencil down and sit quietly.

Put your finger on number 1. Look at the singular word. Now look at the three choices. Find the word that is the plural form of the singular word. (Repeat direction.) Fill in the correct answer circle.

Put your finger on number 2. Look at the singular word. Now look at the three choices. Find the word that is the plural form of the singular word. (Repeat direction.) Fill in the correct answer circle.

Put your finger on number 3. Look at the singular word. Now look at the three choices. Find the word that is the plural form of the singular word. (Repeat direction.) Fill in the correct answer circle.

Put your finger on number 4. Look at the singular word. Now look at the three choices. Find the word that is the plural form of the singular word. (Repeat direction.) Fill in the correct answer circle.

Put your finger on number 5. Look at the singular word. Now look at the three choices. Find the word that is the plural form of the singular word. (Repeat direction.) Fill in the correct answer circle.

Put your finger on number 6. Look at the singular word. Now look at the three choices. Find the word that is the plural form of the singular word. (Repeat direction.) Fill in the correct answer circle.

Put your finger on number 7. Look at the singular word. Now look at the three choices. Find the word that is the plural form of the singular word. (Repeat direction.) Fill in the correct answer circle.

Put your finger on number 8. Look at the singular word. Now look at the three choices. Find the word that is the plural form of the singular word. (Repeat direction.) Fill in the correct answer circle.

Put your finger on number 9. Look at the singular word. Now look at the three choices. Find the word that is the plural form of the singular word. (Repeat direction.) Fill in the correct answer circle.

Put your finger on number 10. Look at the singular word. Now look at the three choices. Find the word that is the plural form of the singular word. (Repeat direction.) Fill in the correct answer circle.

Now we stop.

Answer Key

1.	A	**6.**	C
2.	B	**7.**	B
3.	C	**8.**	C
4.	B	**9.**	A
5.	A	**10.**	B

Plural Nouns

1. movie
   - (A) movies
   - (B) moves
   - (C) movexs

2. berry
   - (A) berrys
   - (B) berries
   - (C) berres

3. lunch
   - (A) lunchies
   - (B) lunchs
   - (C) lunches

4. book
   - (A) bookies
   - (B) books
   - (C) bookxes

5. child
   - (A) children
   - (B) childies
   - (C) childs

6. dress
   - (A) dressies
   - (B) dresss
   - (C) dresses

7. tooth
   - (A) tooths
   - (B) teeth
   - (C) toothies

8. tree
   - (A) treeies
   - (B) trexes
   - (C) trees

9. candy
   - (A) candies
   - (B) candys
   - (C) candixes

10. fly
    - (A) flys
    - (B) flies
    - (C) flixes

STOP

Reproduce and pass out page 47 to students.

Teacher Script

In this test, we are going to practice identifying digraphs. Digraphs are two letters that make a single sound. They can be at the beginning or at the end of a word. I will give you a direction for each picture, and you will fill in the answer. I will not stop to discuss the directions, but I will go slowly enough for you to finish each one. When you are finished, put your pencil down and sit quietly.

Put your finger on the sample. Look at the picture. What is this a picture of? That's right. It's a shoe. Now look at the three choices. You have to find the digraph that's in the word shoe. Which one did you choose? Right again. It's B, because the digraph *sh* begins the word *shoe*. Fill in the correct answer circle. Now let's begin.

Put your finger on number 1. Look at the picture. Find the digraph in this word. Fill in the correct answer circle.

Put your finger on number 2. Look at the picture. Find the digraph in this word. Fill in the correct answer circle.

Put your finger on number 3. Look at the picture. Find the digraph in this word. Fill in the correct answer circle.

Put your finger on number 4. Look at the picture. Find the digraph in this word. Fill in the correct answer circle.

Put your finger on number 5. Look at the picture. Find the digraph in this word. Fill in the correct answer circle.

Put your finger on number 6. Look at the picture. Find the digraph in this word. Fill in the correct answer circle.

Put your finger on number 7. Look at the picture. Find the digraph in this word. Fill in the correct answer circle.

Put your finger on number 8. Look at the picture. Find the digraph in this word. Fill in the correct answer circle.

Put your finger on number 9. Look at the picture. Find the digraph in this word. Fill in the correct answer circle.

Put your finger on number 10. Look at the picture. Find the digraph in this word. Fill in the correct answer circle.

Now we stop.

Answer Key	
1. C	6. B
2. A	7. A
3. C	8. B
4. A	9. A
5. C	10. A

Digraphs

Sample:

- (A) st
- (B) sh
- (C) dr

1.

- (A) br
- (B) sn
- (C) wh

2.

- (A) th
- (B) tr
- (C) st

3.

- (A) bo
- (B) th
- (C) ph

4.

- (A) ch
- (B) st
- (C) tr

5.

- (A) st
- (B) di
- (C) sh

6.

- (A) el
- (B) wh
- (C) dr

7.

- (A) qu
- (B) en
- (C) br

8.

- (A) ki
- (B) ng
- (C) pr

9.

- (A) sh
- (B) fi
- (C) fr

10.

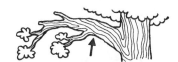

- (A) ch
- (B) ra
- (C) br

Possessives

Reproduce and pass out page 49 to students.

Teacher Script

In this test, we are going to practice identifying possessive nouns. I will give you a direction for each phrase, and you will fill in the answer. I will not stop to discuss the directions, but I will go slowly enough for you to finish each one. When you are finished, put your pencil down and sit quietly.

Put your finger on the sample. Read the phrase. What does it say? Correct. It says *the cat that belongs to Jim.* Now look at the three choices. Which one shows the correct possessive form? That's right. It's C. Fill in the correct answer circle. Now let's begin.

Put your finger on number 1. Read the phrase silently. Now look at the three choices. Find the correct possessive form. Fill in the correct answer circle.

Put your finger on number 2. Read the phrase silently. Now look at the three choices. Find the correct possessive form. Fill in the correct answer circle.

Put your finger on number 3. Read the phrase silently. Now look at the three choices. Find the correct possessive form. Fill in the correct answer circle.

Put your finger on number 4. Read the phrase silently. Now look at the three choices. Find the correct possessive form. Fill in the correct answer circle.

Put your finger on number 5. Read the phrase silently. Now look at the three choices. Find the correct possessive form. Fill in the correct answer circle.

Put your finger on number 6. Read the phrase silently. Now look at the three choices. Find the correct possessive form. Fill in the correct answer circle.

Put your finger on number 7. Read the phrase silently. Now look at the three choices. Find the correct possessive form. Fill in the correct answer circle.

Put your finger on number 8. Read the phrase silently. Now look at the three choices. Find the correct possessive form. Fill in the correct answer circle.

Put your finger on number 9. Read the phrase silently. Now look at the three choices. Find the correct possessive form. Fill in the correct answer circle.

Put your finger on number 10. Read the phrase silently. Now look at the three choices. Find the correct possessive form. Fill in the correct answer circle.

Now we stop.

Answer Key

1. A	6. C
2. B	7. A
3. A	8. B
4. C	9. B
5. A	10. A

Possessives

Sample: the cat that belongs to Jim
- (A) Jims cat
- (B) Jims cat's
- (C) Jim's cat

1. the book that belongs to Mike
   - (A) Mike's book
   - (B) Mikes book
   - (C) Mike's book's

2. the chalk that belongs to the teacher
   - (A) the teachers chalk
   - (B) the teacher's chalk
   - (C) the teachers chalks

3. the apple that belongs to Juan
   - (A) Juan's apple
   - (B) Juans apple
   - (C) Juans apple's

4. the bike that belongs to Amed
   - (A) Ameds bikes
   - (B) Amed's bike's
   - (C) Amed's bike

5. the pen that belongs to my dad
   - (A) my dad's pen
   - (B) my dads pen's
   - (C) my dads pens

6. the toy that belongs to my sister
   - (A) my sisters toys
   - (B) my sister's toys
   - (C) my sister's toy

7. the computer that belongs to the school
   - (A) the school's computer
   - (B) the schools computer's
   - (C) the school's computer's

8. the dish that belongs to my cat
   - (A) my cats dishes
   - (B) my cat's dish
   - (C) my cat's dishe's

9. the glasses that belong to my mother
   - (A) my mothers glasses
   - (B) my mother's glasses
   - (C) my mother's glasse'ss

10. the game that belongs to my friend
    - (A) my friend's game
    - (B) my friends games
    - (C) my friend games

Reproduce and pass out page 51 to students.

Teacher Script

In this test, we are going to practice identifying synonyms. I will give you a direction for each group of words, and you will fill in the answer. I will not stop to discuss the directions, but I will go slowly enough for you to finish each one. When you are finished, put your pencil down and sit quietly. Now let's begin.

Put your finger on number 1. Read the underlined word silently. Now look at the three choices. Find the synonym for the underlined word. Fill in the correct answer circle.

Put your finger on number 2. Read the underlined word silently. Now look at the three choices. Find the synonym for the underlined word. Fill in the correct answer circle.

Put your finger on number 3. Read the underlined word silently. Now look at the three choices. Find the synonym for the underlined word. Fill in the correct answer circle.

Put your finger on number 4. Read the underlined word silently. Now look at the three choices. Find the synonym for the underlined word. Fill in the correct answer circle.

Put your finger on number 5. Read the underlined word silently. Now look at the three choices. Find the synonym for the underlined word. Fill in the correct answer circle.

Put your finger on number 6. Read the underlined word silently. Now look at the three choices. Find the synonym for the underlined word. Fill in the correct answer circle.

Put your finger on number 7. Read the underlined word silently. Now look at the three choices. Find the synonym for the underlined word. Fill in the correct answer circle.

Put your finger on number 8. Read the underlined word silently. Now look at the three choices. Find the synonym for the underlined word. Fill in the correct answer circle.

Put your finger on number 9. Read the underlined word silently. Now look at the three choices. Find the synonym for the underlined word. Fill in the correct answer circle.

Put your finger on number 10. Read the underlined word silently. Now look at the three choices. Find the synonym for the underlined word. Fill in the correct answer circle.

Now we stop.

Answer Key

1.	B	6.	B
2.	C	7.	A
3.	C	8.	B
4.	A	9.	A
5.	A	10.	C

Synonyms

1. <u>loud</u>
   - (A) quiet
   - (B) noisy
   - (C) silent

2. <u>pretty</u>
   - (A) ugly
   - (B) large
   - (C) beautiful

3. <u>happy</u>
   - (A) sad
   - (B) angry
   - (C) glad

4. <u>fast</u>
   - (A) quick
   - (B) slow
   - (C) strong

5. <u>clean</u>
   - (A) tidy
   - (B) dirty
   - (C) fresh

6. <u>shiny</u>
   - (A) dull
   - (B) bright
   - (C) colorful

7. <u>hot</u>
   - (A) warm
   - (B) cold
   - (C) sunny

8. <u>mean</u>
   - (A) nice
   - (B) nasty
   - (C) kind

9. <u>wet</u>
   - (A) soggy
   - (B) dry
   - (C) rough

10. <u>chair</u>
   - (A) bed
   - (B) desk
   - (C) seat

STOP

Reproduce and pass out page 53 to students.

Teacher Script

In this test, we are going to practice identifying antonyms. I will give you a direction for each group of words, and you will fill in the answer. I will not stop to discuss the directions, but I will go slowly enough for you to finish each one. When you are finished, put your pencil down and sit quietly. Now let's begin.

Put your finger on number 1. Read the underlined word silently. Now look at the three choices. Find the antonym for the underlined word. Fill in the correct answer circle.

Put your finger on number 2. Read the underlined word silently. Now look at the three choices. Find the antonym for the underlined word. Fill in the correct answer circle.

Put your finger on number 3. Read the underlined word silently. Now look at the three choices. Find the antonym for the underlined word. Fill in the correct answer circle.

Put your finger on number 4. Read the underlined word silently. Now look at the three choices. Find the antonym for the underlined word. Fill in the correct answer circle.

Put your finger on number 5. Read the underlined word silently. Now look at the three choices. Find the antonym for the underlined word. Fill in the correct answer circle.

Put your finger on number 6. Read the underlined word silently. Now look at the three choices. Find the antonym for the underlined word. Fill in the correct answer circle.

Put your finger on number 7. Read the underlined word silently. Now look at the three choices. Find the antonym for the underlined word. Fill in the correct answer circle.

Put your finger on number 8. Read the underlined word silently. Now look at the three choices. Find the antonym for the underlined word. Fill in the correct answer circle.

Put your finger on number 9. Read the underlined word silently. Now look at the three choices. Find the antonym for the underlined word. Fill in the correct answer circle.

Put your finger on number 10. Read the underlined word silently. Now look at the three choices. Find the antonym for the underlined word. Fill in the correct answer circle.

Now we stop.

Answer Key

1.	A	6.	A
2.	B	7.	C
3.	C	8.	A
4.	B	9.	C
5.	C	10.	B

Antonyms

1. big
   - Ⓐ small
   - Ⓑ large
   - Ⓒ giant-sized

2. cold
   - Ⓐ cool
   - Ⓑ hot
   - Ⓒ freezing

3. smooth
   - Ⓐ soft
   - Ⓑ cracked
   - Ⓒ rough

4. healthy
   - Ⓐ fit
   - Ⓑ sick
   - Ⓒ sad

5. neat
   - Ⓐ tidy
   - Ⓑ clean
   - Ⓒ messy

6. full
   - Ⓐ empty
   - Ⓑ heavy
   - Ⓒ complete

7. rainy
   - Ⓐ wet
   - Ⓑ cold
   - Ⓒ sunny

8. truthful
   - Ⓐ dishonest
   - Ⓑ smart
   - Ⓒ silly

9. hard
   - Ⓐ sticky
   - Ⓑ hot
   - Ⓒ soft

10. long
    - Ⓐ stocky
    - Ⓑ short
    - Ⓒ skinny

STOP

Adverbs and Adjectives

Reproduce and pass out page 55 to students.

Teacher Script

In this test, we are going to practice identifying adverbs and adjectives. I will ask you a question about each sentence, and you will fill in the answer. I will not stop to discuss the questions, but I will go slowly enough for you to finish each one. When you are finished, put your pencil down and sit quietly. Now let's begin.

Put your finger on number 1. Read the sentence silently. Which word in the sentence is an adverb? Look at the three choices. Fill in the correct answer circle.

Put your finger on number 2. Read the sentence silently. Which word in the sentence is an adjective? Look at the three choices. Fill in the correct answer circle.

Put your finger on number 3. Read the sentence silently. Which word in the sentence is an adverb? Look at the three choices. Fill in the correct answer circle.

Put your finger on number 4. Read the sentence silently. Which word in the sentence is an adjective? Look at the three choices. Fill in the correct answer circle.

Put your finger on number 5. Read the sentence silently. Which word in the sentence is an adverb? Look at the three choices. Fill in the correct answer circle.

Put your finger on number 6. Read the sentence silently. Which word in the sentence is an adverb? Look at the three choices. Fill in the correct answer circle.

Put your finger on number 7. Read the sentence silently. Which word in the sentence is an adjective? Look at the three choices. Fill in the correct answer circle.

Put your finger on number 8. Read the sentence silently. Which word in the sentence is an adverb? Look at the three choices. Fill in the correct answer circle.

Put your finger on number 9. Read the sentence silently. Which word in the sentence is an adjective? Look at the three choices. Fill in the correct answer circle.

Put your finger on number 10. Read the sentence silently. Which word in the sentence is an adjective? Look at the three choices. Fill in the correct answer circle.

Now we stop.

Answer Key

1. C	**6.** C
2. B	**7.** A
3. A	**8.** C
4. B	**9.** B
5. A	**10.** C

Adverbs and Adjectives

Adv
1. The students played quietly in the yard.
   - (A) students
   - (B) played
   - Ⓒ quietly

Adv
6. The coach yelled loudly at the players.
   - (A) coach
   - (B) players
   - Ⓒ loudly

Adj
2. My cat is the biggest in the neighborhood.
   - Ⓐ cat
   - Ⓑ biggest
   - (C) the

Adj
7. She is the quickest on the track team.
   - Ⓐ quickest
   - (B) is
   - (C) she

Adv
3. I looked up to see the balloon.
   - Ⓐ up
   - (B) see
   - (C) I

Adv
8. I walked to the park today.
   - (A) park
   - (B) walked
   - Ⓒ today

Adj
4. A tennis ball is smaller than a basketball.
   - (A) is
   - Ⓑ smaller
   - (C) a

Adj
9. The fire alarm is really loud!
   - (A) alarm
   - Ⓑ loud
   - (C) is

Adv
5. My mother told me to come inside for dinner.
   - Ⓐ inside
   - (B) told
   - (C) dinner

Adj *N*   *V*
10. The red in my sweater is the brightest color.
   - (A) color
   - (B) sweater
   - Ⓒ brightest

STOP

Proofing Sentences

Reproduce and pass out page 57 to students.

Teacher Script

In this test, we are going to practice identifying mistakes in sentences. The mistakes could be capitalization, punctuation, or grammar. I will ask you a question about each sentence, and you will fill in the answer. I will not stop to discuss the questions, but I will go slowly enough for you to finish each one. When you are finished, put your pencil down and sit quietly. Now let's begin.

Put your finger on number 1. Read the three sentences silently. Which sentence has no mistakes? (Repeat question.) Fill in the correct answer circle.

Put your finger on number 2. Read the three sentences silently. Which sentence has no mistakes? (Repeat question.) Fill in the correct answer circle.

Put your finger on number 3. Read the three sentences silently. Which sentence has no mistakes? (Repeat question.) Fill in the correct answer circle.

Put your finger on number 4. Read the three sentences silently. Which sentence has no mistakes? (Repeat question.) Fill in the correct answer circle.

Put your finger on number 5. Read the three sentences silently. Which sentence has no mistakes? (Repeat question.) Fill in the correct answer circle.

Put your finger on number 6. Read the three sentences silently. Which sentence has no mistakes? (Repeat question.) Fill in the correct answer circle.

Put your finger on number 7. Read the three sentences silently. Which sentence has no mistakes? (Repeat question.) Fill in the correct answer circle.

Put your finger on number 8. Read the three sentences silently. Which sentence has no mistakes? (Repeat question.) Fill in the correct answer circle.

Put your finger on number 9. Read the three sentences silently. Which sentence has no mistakes? (Repeat question.) Fill in the correct answer circle.

Put your finger on number 10. Read the three sentences silently. Which sentence has no mistakes? (Repeat question.) Fill in the correct answer circle.

Now we stop.

Answer Key

1.	A	**6.**	A
2.	B	**7.**	C
3.	A	**8.**	B
4.	C	**9.**	A
5.	C	**10.**	A

Proofing Sentences

1. (A) I like chocolate ice cream.

   (B) i like chocolate ice cream.

   (C) I like chocolate ice cream?

2. (A) I went to the store with karen.

   (B) I went to the store with Karen.

   (C) i went to the store with Karen.

3. (A) I bought pencils, paper, and erasers.

   (B) I bought pencils paper and erasers.

   (C) I bought pencils paper, and erasers.

4. (A) How many books have you read!

   (B) How many books have you read.

   (C) How many books have you read?

5. (A) We saw a octopus at the zoo.

   (B) We saw and octopus at the zoo.

   (C) We saw an octopus at the zoo.

6. (A) Lucy's cat was up a tree.

   (B) Lucys cat was up a tree.

   (C) Lucy's cat was up an tree.

7. (A) Us had a great time at the water park!

   (B) Them had a great time at the water park!

   (C) We had a great time at the water park!

8. (A) The salad had carrots lettuce and peppers.

   (B) The salad had carrots, lettuce, and peppers.

   (C) The salad had carrots, lettuce and, peppers.

9. (A) George Washington was the first president.

   (B) George washington was the first president.

   (C) george Washington was the first president.

10. (A) May I go to the movies tonight?

    (B) May I go to the movies tonight.

    (C) May I go to the movies tonight!

Contractions

Reproduce and pass out page 59 to students.

Teacher Script

In this test, we are going to practice identifying contractions. I will give you a direction for each group of words, and you will fill in the answer. I will not stop to discuss the directions, but I will go slowly enough for you to finish each one. When you are finished, put your pencil down and sit quietly. First, let's do one together.

Put your finger on the sample. Look at the first two words. What do they say? That's right! They say *I will*. Now look at the three choices. You have to find the contraction for the words *I will*. Which one do you think it is? That's correct. It's B. *I'll* is the contraction for *I will*. Fill in the correct answer circle. Now let's begin.

Put your finger on number 1. Look at the first two words. Find the contraction for these words. Fill in the correct answer circle.

Put your finger on number 2. Look at the first two words. Find the contraction for these words. Fill in the correct answer circle.

Put your finger on number 3. Look at the first two words. Find the contraction for these words. Fill in the correct answer circle.

Put your finger on number 4. Look at the first two words. Find the contraction for these words. Fill in the correct answer circle.

Put your finger on number 5. Look at the first two words. Find the contraction for these words. Fill in the correct answer circle.

Put your finger on number 6. Look at the first two words. Find the contraction for these words. Fill in the correct answer circle.

Put your finger on number 7. Look at the first two words. Find the contraction for these words. Fill in the correct answer circle.

Put your finger on number 8. Look at the first two words. Find the contraction for these words. Fill in the correct answer circle.

Put your finger on number 9. Look at the first two words. Find the contraction for these words. Fill in the correct answer circle.

Put your finger on number 10. Look at the first two words. Find the contraction for these words. Fill in the correct answer circle.

Now we stop.

Answer Key	
1. A	**6.** C
2. B	**7.** A
3. C	**8.** B
4. A	**9.** C
5. B	**10.** A

Contractions

Sample: I will

(A)   It'll

(B)   I'll

(C)   isn't

---

1. has not

(A) hasn't

(B) has'nt

(C) haven't

2. could not

(A) can't

(B) couldn't

(C) wouldn't

3. did not

(A) doesn't

(B) don't

(C) didn't

4. can not

(A) can't

(B) couldn't

(C) ca'nt

5. are not

(A) won't

(B) aren't

(C) can't

6. he will

(A) he'al

(B) she'll

(C) he'll

7. have not

(A) haven't

(B) hasn't

(C) shouldn't

8. I am

(A) Iam

(B) I'm

(C) Ia'm

9. does not

(A) didn't

(B) don't

(C) doesn't

10. is not

(A) isn't

(B) it'll

(C) is'nt

Friendly Letter

Reproduce and pass out page 61 to students along with a sheet of lined paper.

Teacher Script

In this test, we are going to practice the proper way to write a friendly letter. You will read a letter silently. In the letter that you read there will be many mistakes. You will have to rewrite the letter correctly on a sheet of lined paper.

I will know you are finished when I see you sitting quietly with your pencil in front of you.

You may begin.

Answer Key

June 12, 2008

Rosa Jones

124 Carpenter Road

Chicago, Illinois

Dear Rosa,

How are you? It has been a long time since I last saw you. I am writing to share my news with you. I am going to ride in a race to help raise money for the local park on Saturday. Would you like to come? Let me know.

Sincerely,

Linda

---

june 12 2008

rosa Jones

124 carpenter road

chicago illinois

dear Rosa

how are you. it has been a long time since I last saw

you. i am writing to share my news with you. I am

going to ride in a race to help raise money for the local

park on saturday. would you like to come! let me know.

sincerely

linda

Reproduce and pass out page 63 to students.

Teacher Script

In this test, we are going to practice identifying silent letters. I will give you a direction for each group of words, and you will fill in the answer. I will not stop to discuss the directions, but I will go slowly enough for you to finish each one. When you are finished, put your pencil down and sit quietly. First, let's do one together.

Put your finger on the sample. Read the three words silently. Which one of these words contains a silent letter? That's correct—choice B. The word *knob* has a silent *k*. Fill in the correct answer circle. Now let's begin.

Put your finger on number 1. Read the three words silently. Find the word that contains a silent letter. (Repeat direction.) Fill in the correct answer circle.

Put your finger on number 2. Read the three words silently. Find the word that contains a silent letter. (Repeat direction.) Fill in the correct answer circle.

Put your finger on number 3. Read the three words silently. Find the word that contains a silent letter. (Repeat direction.) Fill in the correct answer circle.

Put your finger on number 4. Read the three words silently. Find the word that contains a silent letter. (Repeat direction.) Fill in the correct answer circle.

Put your finger on number 5. Read the three words silently. Find the word that contains a silent letter. (Repeat direction.) Fill in the correct answer circle.

Put your finger on number 6. Read the three words silently. Find the word that contains a silent letter. (Repeat direction.) Fill in the correct answer circle.

Put your finger on number 7. Read the three words silently. Find the word that contains a silent letter. (Repeat direction.) Fill in the correct answer circle.

Put your finger on number 8. Read the three words silently. Find the word that contains a silent letter. (Repeat direction.) Fill in the correct answer circle.

Put your finger on number 9. Read the three words silently. Find the word that contains a silent letter. (Repeat direction.) Fill in the correct answer circle.

Put your finger on number 10. Read the three words silently. Find the word that contains a silent letter. (Repeat direction.) Fill in the correct answer circle.

Now we stop.

Answer Key

1.	C	6.	C
2.	B	7.	B
3.	A	8.	A
4.	B	9.	C
5.	A	10.	A

Silent Letters

Sample: Ⓐ kite
Ⓑ knob
Ⓒ fork

1. Ⓐ sofa
   Ⓑ ball
   Ⓒ ghost

2. Ⓐ music
   Ⓑ night
   Ⓒ pencil

3. Ⓐ half
   Ⓑ spoon
   Ⓒ bus

4. Ⓐ picture
   Ⓑ wrong
   Ⓒ stamp

5. Ⓐ lamb
   Ⓑ play
   Ⓒ sing

6. Ⓐ sleep
   Ⓑ cry
   Ⓒ knee

7. Ⓐ chew
   Ⓑ high
   Ⓒ plant

8. Ⓐ knight
   Ⓑ never
   Ⓒ lamp

9. Ⓐ car
   Ⓑ gum
   Ⓒ comb

10. Ⓐ knit
    Ⓑ drink
    Ⓒ tree

STOP

Reproduce and pass out page 65 to students.

Teacher Script

In this test, we are going to practice identifying the correct verb tense. I will give you a direction for each group of sentences, and you will fill in the answer. I will not stop to discuss the directions, but I will go slowly enough for you to finish each one. When you are finished, put your pencil down and sit quietly. First, let's do one together.

Put your finger on the sample. Read the three sentences silently. Which one of these sentences contains the correct verb tense? That's correct. It's C. *John runs down the street.* Fill in the correct answer circle. Now let's begin.

Put your finger on number 1. Read the three sentences silently. Find the sentence that contains the correct verb tense. (Repeat direction.) Fill in the correct answer circle.

Put your finger on number 2. Read the three sentences silently. Find the sentence that contains the correct verb tense. (Repeat direction.) Fill in the correct answer circle.

Put your finger on number 3. Read the three sentences silently. Find the sentence that contains the correct verb tense. (Repeat direction.) Fill in the correct answer circle.

Put your finger on number 4. Read the three sentences silently. Find the sentence that contains the correct verb tense. (Repeat direction.) Fill in the correct answer circle.

Put your finger on number 5. Read the three sentences silently. Find the sentence that contains the correct verb tense. (Repeat direction.) Fill in the correct answer circle.

Put your finger on number 6. Read the three sentences silently. Find the sentence that contains the correct verb tense. (Repeat direction.) Fill in the correct answer circle.

Put your finger on number 7. Read the three sentences silently. Find the sentence that contains the correct verb tense. (Repeat direction.) Fill in the correct answer circle.

Put your finger on number 8. Read the three sentences silently. Find the sentence that contains the correct verb tense. (Repeat direction.) Fill in the correct answer circle.

Put your finger on number 9. Read the three sentences silently. Find the sentence that contains the correct verb tense. (Repeat direction.) Fill in the correct answer circle.

Put your finger on number 10. Read the three sentences silently. Find the sentence that contains the correct verb tense. (Repeat direction.) Fill in the correct answer circle.

Now we stop.

Answer Key

1. B	6. A
2. A	7. C
3. B	8. A
4. B	9. A
5. C	10. C

Verb Tense

Sample:
(A) John runned down the street.
(B) John run down the street.
(C) John runs down the street.

1. (A) They has school today.
   (B) They have school today.
   (C) They will has school today.

2. (A) Sharon does her homework every night.
   (B) Sharon do her homework every night.
   (C) Sharon will does her homework every night.

3. (A) The baby cry a lot.
   (B) The baby cried a lot.
   (C) They baby will cried a lot.

4. (A) My dad give me a dollar for milk.
   (B) My dad gave me a dollar for milk.
   (C) My dad given me a dollar for milk.

5. (A) He come to the park.
   (B) He coming to the park.
   (C) He came to the park.

6. (A) I see the statue from here.
   (B) I seen the statue from here.
   (C) I saws the statue from here.

7. (A) I be tired today.
   (B) I being tired today.
   (C) I am tired today.

8. (A) The teacher says to take out your pencil.
   (B) The teacher will says to take out your pencil.
   (C) The teacher saying take out your pencil.

9. (A) I went to the county fair.
   (B) I gone to the county fair.
   (C) I be going to the county fair.

10. (A) My mom likes to sang in the choir.
    (B) My mom sanging in the choir.
    (C) My mom sang in the choir.

Reading Comprehension

Reproduce and pass out page 67 to students.

Teacher Script

Now we will read some stories and answer some questions about what we have read. You will read a story silently. After you have finished reading the story, you will read the questions and then fill in the circle next to the right answer. You may look back to the story to find the answers to the questions. Let's do one together.

Put your finger on the sample story. Read the story silently. *(Give students enough time to read.)* Now put your finger on question number 1. Read the question to yourself. Read the three choices. Which one answers the question? That's right—A. The story is mostly about walking to school.

Now put your finger on number 2. Read the question to yourself. Read the three choices. Which one answers the question? That's correct—B. The story says the children talk and tell jokes on their way to school.

Now put your finger on number 3. Read the question to yourself. Read the three choices. Which one answers the question? Right, again! It's C. The story says the children walk past the park and the store on their way to school.

Now we stop. When you're finished, put your pencil down and sit quietly.

Reading Comprehension

Sample:

I walk to school almost every day. My school is close to my home. I walk to school with my friends. We walk past the park. We walk past the store. We always look both ways before we cross the street. We talk on the way to school. Sometimes we like to tell jokes. When we get close to our school, we say good morning to the crossing guard. She helps us to cross a busy street. I like walking to school with my friends! It's a good way to start the day.

1. What is this story about?
   - (A) walking to school
   - (B) crossing the street
   - (C) doing your homework

2. What do the children do on their way to school?
   - (A) fight
   - (B) talk and tell jokes
   - (C) run and play

3. What do the children walk past on their way to school?
   - (A) the movies
   - (B) the fire house
   - (C) the park and the store

Reproduce and pass out pages 69 and 70 to students.

Teacher Script

Now we will read a story and answer some questions by ourselves. You will read the story silently. After you have finished reading, you will read the questions and then fill in the circle next to the right answer. You may look back to the story to find the answers to the questions.

Read the story silently. *(Give students enough time to read.)* Now turn the page.

Put your finger on question number 1. Read the question to yourself. Read the three choices. Fill in the circle that answers the question.

Put your finger on number 2. Read the question to yourself. Read the three choices. Fill in the circle that answers the question.

Put your finger on number 3. Read the question to yourself. Read the three choices. Fill in the circle that answers the question.

Put your finger on number 4. Read the question to yourself. Read the three choices. Fill in the circle that answers the question.

Put your finger on number 5. Read the question to yourself. Read the three choices. Fill in the circle that answers the question.

Put your finger on number 6. Read the question to yourself. Read the three choices. Fill in the circle that answers the question.

Now we stop. When you're finished, put your pencil down and sit quietly.

Answer Key

1. B
2. A
3. C
4. B
5. C
6. B

I have a cat named Thomas. He has gray and white stripes. Thomas is five years old. Thomas sleeps with me every night. He curls up on my pillow right next to my head. I love to fall asleep listening to him purr.

Last week, I woke up in the middle of the night because I heard Thomas sneeze.

"Are you alright?" I asked, but Thomas just sneezed again.

The next day I told my mother.

"I didn't know that cats could sneeze," I said.

"Sure they can," she said. "Thomas might have a cold."

My mother put Thomas in his cage and we took him to see the vet. On the way, Thomas sneezed again and again.

The vet gave Thomas a check-up.

"He's got a cold," the vet said. "Cats can get colds just like people."

"Will he be alright?" I asked.

"Sure," he said.

The vet gave us some medicine for Thomas. He told us that Thomas would start to feel better in a few days.

When we got home my mother gave Thomas his medicine. Then, I took him to my room and tucked him in on his favorite spot on my pillow. His nose was really stuffed and he sneezed a few more times. Soon he fell asleep.

The next day, Thomas slept all day, which is a lot, even for a cat! I was worried.

"Do you think he will be okay?" I asked my mom.

"Sure he will," she said. "You've had colds and you get better, right?"

My mom was right. When I get a cold, I sneeze and get a stuffy nose. I also sleep a lot. I wonder if my mom worries about me when I'm sick the same way I worry about Thomas.

That night, when I went to bed, Thomas crawled into his usual spot. I closed my eyes and suddenly heard his low, rumbling purr. His nose wasn't stuffed anymore. That's when I knew Thomas was getting better!

1. What is this story about?

Ⓐ a child

Ⓑ a sick cat

Ⓒ colds

2. What is the name of the cat in the story?

Ⓐ Thomas

Ⓑ Mittens

Ⓒ It doesn't say.

3. Where does the cat like to sleep?

Ⓐ under the bed

Ⓑ on the bed

Ⓒ on the pillow

4. How do you think the child in the story feels about the cat?

Ⓐ The child likes the cat.

Ⓑ The child loves the cat.

Ⓒ The child feels sorry for the cat.

5. How old is the cat?

Ⓐ one

Ⓑ six

Ⓒ five

6. How does the child know that the cat is getting better?

Ⓐ She can hear the cat's meow.

Ⓑ She can hear the cat's purr.

Ⓒ The cat stops sneezing.

STOP

Reproduce and pass out page 72 to students.

Teacher Script

In this test, we are going to work with place value. I will give you a direction for each numeral, and you will fill in the answer. I will not stop to discuss the directions, but I will go slowly enough for you to finish each one. When you are finished, put your pencil down and sit quietly. First, let's do one together.

Put your finger on the sample. You will see a numeral that has an underlined digit. What is the underlined digit? Yes, it's a 9. Now, what is the value of the 9 in the numeral? Correct, it is 900 because it is in the hundreds place. Fill in the correct answer circle. Now let's begin. I'll know you are finished when your pencil is down and you are sitting quietly.

Put your finger on number 1. Look at the underlined digit in the numeral. Find the value of the underlined digit. Fill in the correct answer circle.

Put your finger on number 2. Look at the underlined digit in the numeral. Find the value of the underlined digit. Fill in the correct answer circle.

Put your finger on number 3. Look at the underlined digit in the numeral. Find the value of the underlined digit. Fill in the correct answer circle.

Put your finger on number 4. Look at the underlined digit in the numeral. Find the value of the underlined digit. Fill in the correct answer circle.

Put your finger on number 5. Look at the underlined digit in the numeral. Find the value of the underlined digit. Fill in the correct answer circle.

Put your finger on number 6. Look at the underlined digit in the numeral. Find the value of the underlined digit. Fill in the correct answer circle.

Put your finger on number 7. Look at the underlined digit in the numeral. Find the value of the underlined digit. Fill in the correct answer circle.

Put your finger on number 8. Look at the underlined digit in the numeral. Find the value of the underlined digit. Fill in the correct answer circle.

Now we will stop.

Answer Key

1. C
2. B
3. A
4. C
5. B
6. A
7. B
8. C

Sample: 9̲87

  (A) 90

  (B) 900

  (C) 9

---

1. 4̲6̲3

  (A) 600

  (B) 6,000

  (C) 60

5. 8̲9̲0

  (A) 900

  (B) 90

  (C) 9

2. 77̲7̲

  (A) 70

  (B) 7

  (C) 700

6. 57̲6̲

  (A) 6

  (B) 60

  (C) 600

3. 2̲0̲9

  (A) 0

  (B) 10

  (C) 100

7. 2̲74

  (A) 2,000

  (B) 200

  (C) 20

4. 1̲23

  (A) 10

  (B) 1

  (C) 100

8. 63̲2̲

  (A) 200

  (B) 20

  (C) 2

STOP

Reproduce and pass out page 74 to students.

Teacher Script

In this test, we are going to practice using our number sense. I will give you a direction for each series of numbers, and you will fill in the answer. I will not stop to discuss the directions, but I will go slowly enough for you to finish each one. When you are finished, put your pencil down and sit quietly. Now let's begin.

Put your finger on number 1. Find the missing number in the series of numbers. Fill in the correct answer circle.

Put your finger on number 2. Find the missing number in the series of numbers. Fill in the correct answer circle.

Put your finger on number 3. Find the missing number in the series of numbers. Fill in the correct answer circle.

Put your finger on number 4. Find the missing number in the series of numbers. Fill in the correct answer circle.

Put your finger on number 5. Find the missing number in the series of numbers. Fill in the correct answer circle.

Put your finger on number 6. Find the missing number in the series of numbers. Fill in the correct answer circle.

Put your finger on number 7. Find the missing number in the series of numbers. Fill in the correct answer circle.

Put your finger on number 8. Find the missing number in the series of numbers. Fill in the correct answer circle.

Put your finger on number 9. Find the missing number in the series of numbers. Fill in the correct answer circle.

Put your finger on number 10. Find the missing number in the series of numbers. Fill in the correct answer circle.

Now we will stop.

Answer Key	
1. A	**6.** C
2. B	**7.** A
3. C	**8.** C
4. A	**9.** B
5. A	**10.** A

Number Sense

1. 733, _____, 735

(A) 734

(B) 732

(C) 736

2. _____, 238, 239

(A) 236

(B) 237

(C) 240

3. 899, _____, 901

(A) 800

(B) 902

(C) 900

4. 732, 731, _____

(A) 730

(B) 729

(C) 733

5. _____, 504, 503

(A) 505

(B) 506

(C) 502

6. 107, _____, 109

(A) 106

(B) 110

(C) 108

7. 500, _____, 498

(A) 499

(B) 501

(C) 949

8. _____, 300, 301

(A) 399

(B) 303

(C) 299

9. 998, 999, _____

(A) 997

(B) 1,000

(C) 100

10. 498, 499, _____

(A) 500

(B) 497

(C) 501

STOP

Two-Digit Addition and Subtraction

Reproduce and pass out page 76 to students.

Teacher Script

In this test, we are going to practice two-digit addition and subtraction. I will give you a direction for each math problem, and you will fill in the answer. I will not stop to discuss the directions, but I will go slowly enough for you to finish each one. When you are finished, put your pencil down and sit quietly. Now let's begin.

Put your finger on number 1. Find the sum. Fill in the correct answer circle.

Put your finger on number 2. Find the difference. Fill in the correct answer circle.

Put your finger on number 3. Find the difference. Fill in the correct answer circle.

Put your finger on number 4. Find the sum. Fill in the correct answer circle.

Put your finger on number 5. Find the sum. Fill in the correct answer circle.

Put your finger on number 6. Find the difference. Fill in the correct answer circle.

Put your finger on number 7. Find the difference. Fill in the correct answer circle.

Put your finger on number 8. Find the sum. Fill in the correct answer circle.

Put your finger on number 9. Find the sum. Fill in the correct answer circle.

Put your finger on number 10. Find the difference. Fill in the correct answer circle.

Now we will stop.

Answer Key

1.	B	6.	B
2.	B	7.	C
3.	A	8.	A
4.	C	9.	B
5.	A	10.	A

Two-Digit Addition and Subtraction

1.

1

73
+ 18

91

Ⓐ 90
Ⓑ 91
Ⓒ 55

6.

5

64 \4
− 47

17

Ⓐ 71
Ⓑ 17
Ⓒ 111

2.

188
− 29

59

Ⓐ 95
Ⓑ 59
Ⓒ 117

7.

7.10

80
− 35

45

Ⓐ 54
Ⓑ 115
Ⓒ 45

3.

32
− 24

8

Ⓐ 8
Ⓑ 56
Ⓒ 18

8.

63
+ 53

116

Ⓐ 116
Ⓑ 611
Ⓒ 45

4.

1

57
+ 39

96

Ⓐ 69
Ⓑ 18
Ⓒ 96

9.

1

29
+ 12

41

Ⓐ 14
Ⓑ 41
Ⓒ 17

5.

92
+ 17

109

Ⓐ 109
Ⓑ 911
Ⓒ 65

10.

74
− 65

9

Ⓐ 9
Ⓑ 139
Ⓒ 10

Three-Digit Addition and Subtraction 1

Reproduce and pass out page 78 to students.

Teacher Script

In this test, we are going to practice three-digit addition and subtraction. I will give you a direction for each math problem, and you will fill in the answer. I will not stop to discuss the directions, but I will go slowly enough for you to finish each one. When you are finished, put your pencil down and sit quietly. Now let's begin.

Put your finger on number 1. Find the sum. Fill in the correct answer circle.

Put your finger on number 2. Find the difference. Fill in the correct answer circle.

Put your finger on number 3. Find the difference. Fill in the correct answer circle.

Put your finger on number 4. Find the sum. Fill in the correct answer circle.

Put your finger on number 5. Find the difference. Fill in the correct answer circle.

Put your finger on number 6. Find the sum. Fill in the correct answer circle.

Put your finger on number 7. Find the difference. Fill in the correct answer circle.

Put your finger on number 8. Find the sum. Fill in the correct answer circle.

Put your finger on number 9. Find the difference. Fill in the correct answer circle.

Put your finger on number 10. Find the sum. Fill in the correct answer circle.

Now we will stop.

Answer Key

1.	A	6.	B
2.	B	7.	C
3.	C	8.	C
4.	A	9.	A
5.	B	10.	B

Three-Digit Addition and Subtraction 1

1.

$$809 + 128$$
937

(A) 937
(B) 739
(C) 763

6.

$$563 + 318$$
881

(A) 818
(B) 881
(C) 811

2.

$$763 - 671$$
092

(A) 29
(B) 92
(C) 28

7.

$$337 - 246$$
091

(A) 19
(B) 20
(C) 91

3.

$$809 - 522$$
287

(A) 782
(B) 872
(C) 287

8.

$$572 + 372$$
944

(A) 449
(B) 943
(C) 944

4.

$$774 + 182$$
956

(A) 956
(B) 569
(C) 955

9.

$$624 - 483$$
141

(A) 141
(B) 107
(C) 147

5.

$$407 - 216$$
191

(A) 911
(B) 191
(C) 119

10.

$$535 + 296$$
831

(A) 239
(B) 831
(C) 813

Three-Digit Addition and Subtraction 2

Reproduce and pass out page 80 to students.

Teacher Script

In this test, we are going to practice three-digit addition and subtraction. I will give you a direction for each math problem, and you will fill in the answer. I will not stop to discuss the directions, but I will go slowly enough for you to finish each one. When you are finished, put your pencil down and sit quietly. Now let's begin.

Put your finger on number 1. Find the sum. Fill in the correct answer circle.

Put your finger on number 2. Find the difference. Fill in the correct answer circle.

Put your finger on number 3. Find the difference. Fill in the correct answer circle.

Put your finger on number 4. Find the sum. Fill in the correct answer circle.

Put your finger on number 5. Find the sum. Fill in the correct answer circle.

Put your finger on number 6. Find the difference. Fill in the correct answer circle.

Put your finger on number 7. Find the difference. Fill in the correct answer circle.

Put your finger on number 8. Find the sum. Fill in the correct answer circle.

Put your finger on number 9. Find the sum. Fill in the correct answer circle.

Put your finger on number 10. Find the difference. Fill in the correct answer circle.

Now we will stop.

Answer Key

1.	A	6.	B
2.	B	7.	C
3.	C	8.	A
4.	A	9.	C
5.	C	10.	B

Three-Digit Addition and Subtraction 2

1.

$$\begin{array}{r} \overset{1}{732} \\ + 139 \\ \hline 871 \end{array}$$

- (A) 871
- (B) 781
- (C) 593

2.

$$\begin{array}{r} \overset{-10}{406} \\ - 391 \\ \hline 15 \end{array}$$

- (A) 51
- (B) 15
- (C) 797

3.

$$\begin{array}{r} \overset{-15}{852} \\ - 762 \\ \hline 090 \end{array}$$

- (A) 9
- (B) 449
- (C) 90

4.

$$\begin{array}{r} \overset{1}{219} \\ + 179 \\ \hline 398 \end{array}$$

- (A) 398
- (B) 893
- (C) 397

5.

$$\begin{array}{r} \overset{1}{507} \\ + 407 \\ \hline 914 \end{array}$$

- (A) 419
- (B) 149
- (C) 914

6.

$$\begin{array}{r} \overset{-15}{459} \\ - 361 \\ \hline 98 \end{array}$$

- (A) 89
- (B) 98
- (C) 115

7.

$$\begin{array}{r} \overset{-12}{382} \\ - 253 \\ \hline 129 \end{array}$$

- (A) 128
- (B) 130
- (C) 129

8.

$$\begin{array}{r} 433 \\ + 323 \\ \hline 756 \end{array}$$

- (A) 756
- (B) 507
- (C) 749

9.

$$\begin{array}{r} \overset{1}{737} \\ + 127 \\ \hline 864 \end{array}$$

- (A) 648
- (B) 848
- (C) 864

10.

$$\begin{array}{r} \overset{13}{132} \\ - 90 \\ \hline 42 \end{array}$$

- (A) 24
- (B) 42
- (C) 40

Identifying Numbers

Reproduce and pass out page 82 to students.

Teacher Script

In this test, we are going to practice identifying number words and numerals. I will give you a direction for each set of numbers, and you will fill in the answer. I will not stop to discuss the directions, but I will go slowly enough for you to finish each one. When you are finished, put your pencil down and sit quietly. Now let's begin.

Put your finger on number 1. Find the word for the numeral shown. Fill in the correct answer circle.

Put your finger on number 2. Find the numeral for the word shown. Fill in the correct answer circle.

Put your finger on number 3. Find the numeral for the word shown. Fill in the correct answer circle.

Put your finger on number 4. Find the word for the numeral shown. Fill in the correct answer circle.

Put your finger on number 5. Find the word for the numeral shown. Fill in the correct answer circle.

Put your finger on number 6. Find the numeral for the word shown. Fill in the correct answer circle.

Put your finger on number 7. Find the word for the amount shown. Fill in the correct answer circle.

Put your finger on number 8. Find the word for the amount shown. Fill in the correct answer circle.

Put your finger on number 9. Find the word for the amount shown. Fill in the correct answer circle.

Put your finger on number 10. Find the word for the amount shown. Fill in the correct answer circle.

Put your finger on number 11. Find the word for the amount shown. Fill in the correct answer circle.

Put your finger on number 12. Find the word for the amount shown. Fill in the correct answer circle.

Now we will stop.

Answer Key

1.	A	7.	A
2.	B	8.	C
3.	C	9.	A
4.	B	10.	C
5.	A	11.	A
6.	C	12.	C

Identifying Numbers

1. 80
   - (A) eighty
   - (B) eight
   - (C) eigt

2. fifty-two
   - (A) 50
   - (B) 52
   - (C) 500

3. twelve
   - (A) 20
   - (B) 21
   - (C) 12

4. 77
   - (A) seven
   - (B) seventy-seven
   - (C) seventie

5. 48
   - (A) forty-eight
   - (B) forty-eigt
   - (C) four

6. thirty-five
   - (A) 30
   - (B) 53
   - (C) 35

7. 7 tens and 5 ones
   - (A) seventy-five
   - (B) seventy
   - (C) fifty-seven

8. 1 ten and 3 ones
   - (A) ten
   - (B) fourteen
   - (C) thirteen

9. 17 ones
   - (A) seventeen
   - (B) seven
   - (C) seventy

10. 62 ones
    - (A) twenty-six
    - (B) sixty
    - (C) sixty-two

11. 10 tens
    - (A) one hundred
    - (B) fifty
    - (C) ten

12. 2 tens and 8 ones
    - (A) eighty-two
    - (B) twenty-two
    - (C) twenty-eight

STOP

Counting Money

Reproduce and pass out page 84 to students.

Teacher Script

Now it's time to practice counting money. I will give you a direction for each set of coins, and you will fill in the answer. I will not stop to discuss the directions, but I will go slowly enough for you to finish each one. When you are finished, put your pencil down and sit quietly. Now let's begin.

Put your finger on number 1. Count the money. Fill in the correct answer circle.

Put your finger on number 2. Count the money. Fill in the correct answer circle.

Put your finger on number 3. Count the money. Fill in the correct answer circle.

Put your finger on number 4. Count the money. Fill in the correct answer circle.

Put your finger on number 5. Count the money. Fill in the correct answer circle.

Put your finger on number 6. Count the money. Fill in the correct answer circle.

Put your finger on number 7. Count the money. Fill in the correct answer circle.

Put your finger on number 8. Count the money. Fill in the correct answer circle.

Now we will stop.

Answer Key

1. A
2. C
3. A
4. C
5. B
6. C
7. A
8. B

Counting Money

1.

Ⓐ 35 cents Ⓑ 15 cents Ⓒ 20 cents

5.

Ⓐ $1.10 Ⓑ $1.13 Ⓒ $1.00

2.

Ⓐ 28 cents Ⓑ 80 cents Ⓒ 82 cents

6.

Ⓐ 40¢ Ⓑ 47¢ Ⓒ 48¢

3.

Ⓐ $2.25 Ⓑ $2.00 Ⓒ $2.50

7.

Ⓐ $3.28 Ⓑ $3.00 Ⓒ $1.03

4.

Ⓐ 30¢ Ⓑ 7¢ Ⓒ 35¢

8.

Ⓐ 40¢ Ⓑ 47¢ Ⓒ 27¢

Problem Solving with Money

Reproduce and pass out page 86 to students.

Teacher Script

Now we are going to solve some word problems about money. When you solve word problems, it is important to read the problem carefully. You can read the problem more than once if you need to. Look at all of the answer choices before you make a selection. When you are finished, put your pencil down and sit quietly. Now we will begin.

Put your finger on number 1. Read the problem carefully. Look at the three choices. Fill in the correct answer circle.

Put your finger on number 2. Read the problem carefully. Look at the three choices. Fill in the correct answer circle.

Put your finger on number 3. Read the problem carefully. Look at the three choices. Fill in the correct answer circle.

Put your finger on number 4. Read the problem carefully. Look at the three choices. Fill in the correct answer circle.

Put your finger on number 5. Read the problem carefully. Look at the three choices. Fill in the correct answer circle.

Put your finger on number 6. Read the problem carefully. Look at the three choices. Fill in the correct answer circle.

Put your finger on number 7. Read the problem carefully. Look at the three choices. Fill in the correct answer circle.

Put your finger on number 8. Read the problem carefully. Look at the three choices. Fill in the correct answer circle.

Now we will stop.

Answer Key
1. A
2. B
3. C
4. B
5. C
6. C
7. A
8. C

Problem Solving with Money

1. Mike has 3 quarters and 1 nickel. He bought an ice cream bar for 50 cents. How much money does he have left?

   (A) 30 cents   (B) 10 cents   (C) 50 cents

2. Gina has $3.47. She bought a birthday card for $1.50. How much money does she have now?

   (A) $1.50   (B) $1.97   (C) $2.50

3. Rosa has 2 quarters and 2 dimes, which equals 70 cents. Which is another way to make 70 cents?

   (A) 7 nickels   (B) 7 pennies   (C) 7 dimes

4. Marcus has 3 quarters and 4 nickels. What is another way to show this same amount?

   (A) 10 dimes   (B) 9 dimes and 5 pennies   (C) 75 pennies

5. Sharnice has $2.47 in change in a pocket that has a hole in it. If 52¢ falls out, how much money will she have left?

   (A) $1.77   (B) $1.97   (C) $1.95

6. A new comic book costs five dollars and fifty cents. Malcolm has three dollars and twenty-seven cents. George has two dollars and twenty-five cents. If they put their money together how much will they have?

   (A) $5.50   (B) $4.50   (C) $5.52

7. Jennifer has 7 dimes and 1 nickel. What is another way to show this same amount?

   (A) 3 quarters   (B) 4 quarters   (C) 1 dollar coin and 5 pennies

8. Anton has been collecting pennies in a jar for a month. So far he has collected 700 pennies. How many dollars is that?

   (A) $4.00   (B) $8.00   (C) $7.00

STOP

Geometry 1

Reproduce and pass out page 88 to students.

Teacher Script

Now we are going to do some work with geometry. I will ask you a question about each shape, and you will fill in the answer. I will not stop to discuss the questions, but I will go slowly enough for you to finish each one. When you are finished, put your pencil down and sit quietly. Now let's begin.

Put your finger on number 1. What is the name of this figure? Fill in the correct answer circle.

Put your finger on number 2. What is the name of this figure? Fill in the correct answer circle.

Put your finger on number 3. What is the name of this figure? Fill in the correct answer circle.

Put your finger on number 4. What is the name of this figure? Fill in the correct answer circle.

Put your finger on number 5. What is the name of this figure? Fill in the correct answer circle.

Put your finger on number 6. How many vertices does this figure have? Fill in the correct answer circle.

Put your finger on number 7. How many vertices does this figure have? Fill in the correct answer circle.

Put your finger on number 8. How many flat surfaces does this figure have? Fill in the correct answer circle.

Put your finger on number 9. How many edges does this figure have? Fill in the correct answer circle.

Put your finger on number 10. If you folded this shape pattern, what figure would you have? Fill in the correct answer circle.

Now we will stop. I'll know you're finished when your pencil is down and you're sitting quietly.

Answer Key	
1. A	**6.** B
2. C	**7.** A
3. B	**8.** C
4. B	**9.** A
5. B	**10.** B

1.

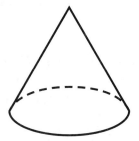

Ⓐ cone

Ⓑ cylinder

Ⓒ pyramid

2.

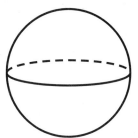

Ⓐ prism

Ⓑ cube

Ⓒ sphere

3.

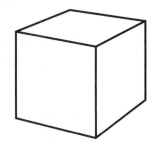

Ⓐ square

Ⓑ cube

Ⓒ rectangular prism

4.

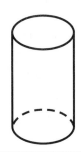

Ⓐ triangle

Ⓑ cylinder

Ⓒ cone

5.

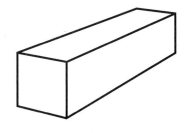

Ⓐ rectangle

Ⓑ rectangular prism

Ⓒ cube

6.

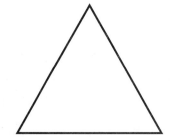

Ⓐ 4

Ⓑ 3

Ⓒ 2

7.

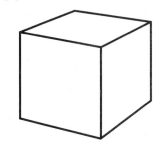

Ⓐ 8

Ⓑ 12

Ⓒ 4

8.

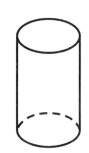

Ⓐ 6

Ⓑ 1

Ⓒ 2

9.

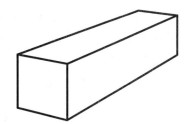

Ⓐ 12

Ⓑ 16

Ⓒ 10

10.

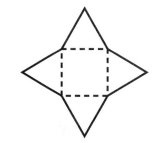

Ⓐ triangle

Ⓑ pyramid

Ⓒ cube

Geometry 2

Reproduce and pass out page 90 to students.

Teacher Script

Now we are going to do some work with geometry. I will ask you a question about each set of shapes, and you will fill in the answer. I will not stop to discuss the questions, but I will go slowly enough for you to finish each one. When you are finished, put your pencil down and sit quietly. Now let's begin.

Put your finger on number 1. Which figure is congruent with the given figure? Fill in the correct answer circle.

Put your finger on number 2. Which figure is congruent with the given figure? Fill in the correct answer circle.

Put your finger on number 3. Which figure is congruent with the given figure? Fill in the correct answer circle.

Put your finger on number 4. Which figure is **not** congruent with the given figure? Fill in the correct answer circle.

Put your finger on number 5. Which figure is **not** congruent with the given figure? Fill in the correct answer circle.

Put your finger on number 6. Has this figure been flipped, slid, or turned? Fill in the correct answer circle.

Put your finger on number 7. Has this figure been flipped, slid, or turned? Fill in the correct answer circle.

Put your finger on number 8. Has this figure been flipped, slid, or turned? Fill in the correct answer circle.

Put your finger on number 9. Which figure has symmetry? Fill in the correct answer circle.

Put your finger on number 10. Which figure has symmetry? Fill in the correct answer circle.

Now we will stop.

Answer Key

1.	C	**6.**	A
2.	C	**7.**	C
3.	A	**8.**	B
4.	B	**9.**	C
5.	A	**10.**	B

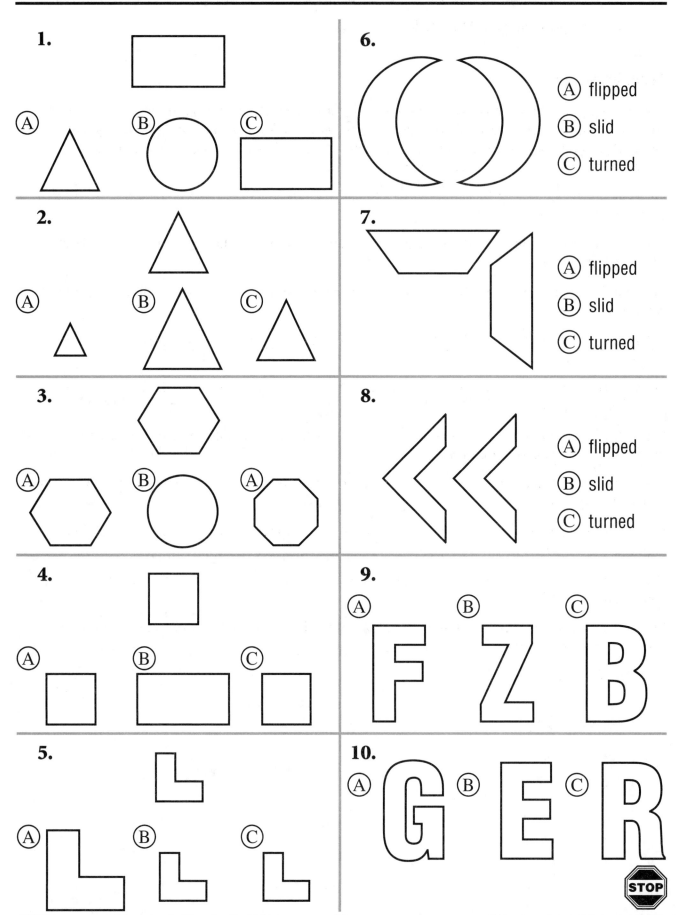

1.

Ⓐ Ⓑ Ⓒ

2.

Ⓐ Ⓑ Ⓒ

3.

Ⓐ Ⓑ Ⓐ

4.

Ⓐ Ⓑ Ⓒ

5.

Ⓐ Ⓑ Ⓒ

6.

Ⓐ flipped

Ⓑ slid

Ⓒ turned

7.

Ⓐ flipped

Ⓑ slid

Ⓒ turned

8.

Ⓐ flipped

Ⓑ slid

Ⓒ turned

9.

Ⓐ Ⓑ Ⓒ

F Z B

10.

Ⓐ G Ⓑ E Ⓒ R

Measurement 1

Reproduce and pass out page 92 to students.

Teacher Script

Now we are going to do some work with measurement. You will read most of the questions to yourself. I will ask you a few of the questions, and you will fill in the answers. I will not stop to discuss the questions, but I will go slowly enough for you to finish each one. When you are finished, put your pencil down and sit quietly. Now let's begin.

Put your finger on number 1. Read the question silently. Now read the three choices. Fill in the correct answer circle.

Put your finger on number 2. Read the question silently. Now read the three choices. Fill in the correct answer circle.

Put your finger on number 3. Read the question silently. Now read the three choices. Fill in the correct answer circle.

Put your finger on number 4. Read the question silently. Now read the three choices. Fill in the correct answer circle.

Put your finger on number 5. Read the question silently. Now read the three choices. Fill in the correct answer circle.

Put your finger on number 6. In real life, which one of these objects has the greatest capacity? Fill in the correct answer circle.

Put your finger on number 7. In real life, which one of these objects is the shortest? Fill in the correct answer circle.

Put your finger on number 8. Read the question silently. Now read the three choices. Fill in the correct answer circle.

Put your finger on number 9. Read the question silently. Now read the three choices. Fill in the correct answer circle.

Put your finger on number 10. In real life, about how tall do you think this object is? Fill in the correct answer circle.

Now we will stop.

Answer Key

1. B	6. B
2. A	7. C
3. C	8. B
4. B	9. C
5. A	10. B

1. How many inches are in 1 foot?

Ⓐ 10

Ⓑ 12

Ⓒ 8

2. How many feet are in one yard?

Ⓐ 3

Ⓑ 7

Ⓒ 6

3. How many inches are in 1 yard?

Ⓐ 24

Ⓑ 62

Ⓒ 36

4. How many cups are in 1 quart?

Ⓐ 2

Ⓑ 4

Ⓒ 6

5. How many pints are in a quart?

Ⓐ 2

Ⓑ 4

Ⓒ 6

6.

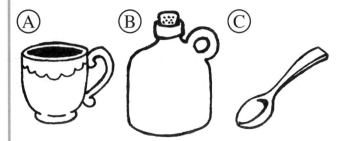

Ⓐ   Ⓑ   Ⓒ

7.

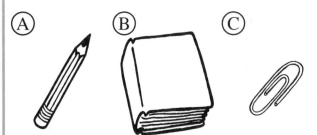

Ⓐ   Ⓑ   Ⓒ

8. What is the perimeter of this rectangle?

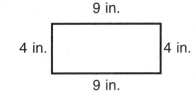

9 in.

4 in.   4 in.

9 in.

Ⓐ 16 in.

Ⓑ 26 in.

Ⓒ 12 in.

9. What is the area of this rectangle?

8 units

3 units

Ⓐ 26 square units

Ⓑ 4 square units

Ⓒ 24 square units

10.

Ⓐ 30 inches

Ⓑ 30 feet

Ⓒ 30 pints

Measurement 2

Reproduce and pass out page 94 to students.

Teacher Script

Now we are going to do some work with measurement. Follow along with me as I give you directions for each number. You will fill in the answers. I will not stop to discuss the questions, but I will go slowly enough for you to finish each one. When you are finished, put your pencil down and sit quietly. Now let's begin.

Put your finger on number 1. Read the question silently. Now read the three choices. Fill in the correct answer circle.

Put your finger on number 2. Which object is the heaviest? Fill in the correct answer circle.

Put your finger on number 3. Which object is the lightest? Fill in the correct answer circle.

Put your finger on number 4. Look at the thermometer. What is the temperature? Fill in the correct answer circle.

Put your finger on number 5. Look at the thermometer. What is the temperature? Fill in the correct answer circle.

Put your finger on number 6. Read the question silently. Now read the three choices. Fill in the correct answer circle.

Put your finger on number 7. Read the question silently. Now read the three choices. Fill in the correct answer circle.

Put your finger on number 8. In real life, about how much do you think this object weighs? Fill in the correct answer circle.

Now we will stop.

Answer Key
1. C
2. A
3. C
4. A
5. C
6. A
7. B
8. B

1. How many ounces are in 1 pound?

   (A) 10

   (B) 14

   (C) 16

2.

(A)   (B)   (C)

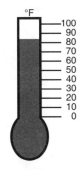

3.

(A)   (B)   (C)

4.

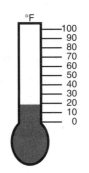

   (A) 83 degrees F

   (B) 80 degrees F

   (C) 90 degrees F

5.

   (A) 20 degrees F

   (B) 15 degrees F

   (C) 19 degrees F

6. The temperature outside is 30 degrees F. What will you be wearing?

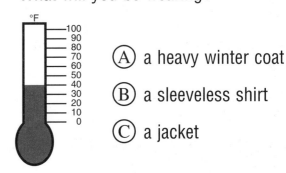

   (A) a heavy winter coat

   (B) a sleeveless shirt

   (C) a jacket

7. The temperature outside is 85 degrees F. What will you be wearing?

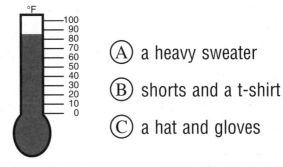

   (A) a heavy sweater

   (B) shorts and a t-shirt

   (C) a hat and gloves

8.

   (A) 5 pounds

   (B) 50 pounds

   (C) 50 ounces

Reproduce and pass out page 96 to students.

Teacher Script

Now we are going to practice telling time. You will read each question silently and then fill in the answer. I will not stop to discuss the questions, but I will go slowly enough for you to answer each one. When you are finished, put your pencil down and sit quietly. Now let's begin.

Put your finger on number 1. Read the question silently. Look at the clock. Fill in the correct answer circle.

Put your finger on number 2. Read the question silently. Look at the clock. Fill in the correct answer circle.

Put your finger on number 3. Read the question silently. Look at the clock. Fill in the correct answer circle.

Put your finger on number 4. Read the question silently. Look at the clock. Fill in the correct answer circle.

Put your finger on number 5. Read the question silently. Look at the clock. Fill in the correct answer circle.

Put your finger on number 6. Read the question silently. Look at the clock. Fill in the correct answer circle.

Put your finger on number 7. Read the question silently. Look at the clock. Fill in the correct answer circle.

Put your finger on number 8. Read the question silently. Look at the clock. Fill in the correct answer circle.

Put your finger on number 9. Read the question silently. Look at the three choices. Fill in the correct answer circle.

Put your finger on number 10. Read the question silently. Look at the three choices. Fill in the correct answer circle.

Now we will stop.

Answer Key

1. B	6. B
2. C	7. A
3. A	8. A
4. B	9. C
5. A	10. A

Time

1. What time is it?

(A) 8:00

(B) 8:05

(C) 8:01

2. What time is it?

(A) 6:04

(B) 6:00

(C) 6:20

3. What time is it?

(A) 9:30

(B) 9:00

(C) 9:06

4. What time is it?

(A) 3:11

(B) 3:55

(C) 3:00

5. What time is it?

(A) quarter to 8

(B) 8:45

(C) half past 8

6. What time is it?

(A) 11:03

(B) quarter past 11

(C) quarter to 11

7. What time is it?

(A) half past 10

(B) quarter past 10

(C) 10:06

8. What time is it?

(A) quarter to 7

(B) 7:45

(C) 6:09

9. It is half past 6. What time will it be in 30 minutes?

(A) 7:30

(B) 6:30

(C) 7:00

10. It is quarter past 1. What time will it be in 15 minutes?

(A) 1:30

(B) 1:15

(C) 1:45

STOP

Reproduce and pass out pages 98 through 100 to students.

Teacher Script

Now we are going to work with graphs and data. You will read each question silently and then fill in the answer. I will not stop to discuss the questions, but I will go slowly enough for you to finish each one. When you are finished, put your pencil down and sit quietly. Now let's begin.

Put your finger on the tally sheet. Look at it carefully. You are going to use this tally sheet to help you answer questions 1 through 4.

Put your finger on number 1. Read the question silently. Read the three choices. Fill in the correct answer circle.

Put your finger on number 2. Read the question silently. Read the three choices. Fill in the correct answer circle.

Put your finger on number 3. Read the question silently. Read the three choices. Fill in the correct answer circle.

Put your finger on number 4. Read the question silently. Read the three choices. Fill in the correct answer circle.

Turn the page.

Put your finger on the Venn diagram. Look at it carefully. You are going to use this Venn diagram to help you answer questions 5 and 6.

Put your finger on number 5. Read the question silently. Read the three choices. Fill in the correct answer circle.

Put your finger on number 6. Read the question silently. Read the three choices. Fill in the correct answer circle.

Now put your finger on the pictograph. Look at it carefully. You are going to use this pictograph to help you answer questions 7 through 9.

Put your finger on number 7. Read the question silently. Read the three choices. Fill in the correct answer circle.

Put your finger on number 8. Read the question silently. Read the three choices. Fill in the correct answer circle.

Put your finger on number 9. Read the question silently. Read the three choices. Fill in the correct answer circle.

Turn the page.

Put your finger on the bar graph. Look at it carefully. You are going to use this bar graph to help you answer questions 10 and 11.

Put your finger on number 10. Read the question silently. Read the three choices. Fill in the correct answer circle.

Put your finger on number 11. Read the question silently. Read the three choices. Fill in the correct answer circle.

Now put your finger on the line plot. Look at it carefully. You are going to use this line plot to help you answer questions 12 and 13.

Put your finger on number 12. Read the question silently. Read the three choices. Fill in the correct answer circle.

Put your finger on number 13. Read the question silently. Read the three choices. Fill in the correct answer circle.

Now we will stop.

Answer Key

1. A	**6.** B	**11.** B
2. C	**7.** A	**12.** C
3. B	**8.** C	**13.** C
4. B	**9.** A	
5. A	**10.** A	

Data

Use this tally sheet to answer questions 1 through 4.

Favorite Fruit	
Type	**Number**
Apples	ЖІ ЖІ ІІ
Peaches	ЖІ ІІІ
Bananas	ІІІ
Grapes	ЖІ ЖІ І
Pears	ІІІІ

1. Which fruit is the most popular?

   (A) apples

   (B) pears

   (C) peaches

2. Which fruit is the least popular?

   (A) grapes

   (B) apples

   (C) bananas

3. How many people liked apples?

   (A) 5

   (B) 12

   (C) 10

4. How many more people liked grapes than bananas?

   (A) 9

   (B) 8

   (C) 11

Use this Venn diagram to answer questions 5 and 6.

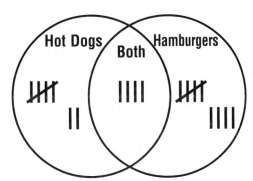

5. How many people just like hot dogs?

Ⓐ 7

Ⓑ 5

Ⓒ 4

6. How many people like hot dogs and hamburgers?

Ⓐ 5

Ⓑ 4

Ⓒ 9

Use this pictograph to answer questions 7 through 9.

Favorite Types of Games	
Board Games	▢ ▢ ▢ ▢
Card Games	▢ ▢
Computer Games	▢ ▢ ▢ ▢ ▢ ▢
Puzzles	▢ ▢ ▢

▢ = 2 kids

7. How many kids liked board games?

Ⓐ 8

Ⓑ 4

Ⓒ 12

9. How many more kids liked puzzles than card games?

Ⓐ 2

Ⓑ 6

Ⓒ 1

8. Which type of game is the most popular?

Ⓐ puzzles

Ⓑ card games

Ⓒ computer games

Use this bar graph to answer questions 10 and 11.

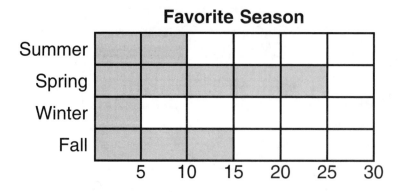

Favorite Season

---

10. Which season is the most popular?

Ⓐ spring

Ⓑ summer

Ⓒ fall

11. How many people like fall and winter altogether?

Ⓐ 25

Ⓑ 20

Ⓒ 15

Use this line plot to answer questions 12 and 13.

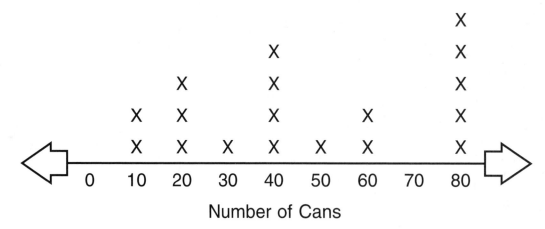

Cans Collected in October

Number of Cans

---

12. How many people collected 40 cans?

Ⓐ 3

Ⓑ 5

Ⓒ 4

13. How many people collected cans altogether?

Ⓐ 15

Ⓑ 20

Ⓒ 18

Reproduce and pass out page 102 to students.

Teacher Script

Now we are going to answer some questions about our solar system. You will read each question silently and then fill in the answer. I will not stop to discuss the questions, but I will go slowly enough for you to finish each one. When you are finished, put your pencil down and sit quietly. Now let's begin.

Put your finger on number 1. Read the question silently. Now read the three choices. Select the choice that answers the question. Fill in the answer circle.

Put your finger on number 2. Read the question silently. Now read the three choices. Select the choice that answers the question. Fill in the answer circle.

Put your finger on number 3. Read the question silently. Now read the three choices. Select the choice that answers the question. Fill in the answer circle.

Put your finger on number 4. Read the question silently. Now read the three choices. Select the choice that answers the question. Fill in the answer circle.

Put your finger on number 5. Read the question silently. Now read the three choices. Select the choice that answers the question. Fill in the answer circle.

Put your finger on number 6. Here there is a blank that you must fill in. Read the sentence silently. Now read the three choices. Select the choice that best completes the sentence. Fill in the answer circle.

Put your finger on number 7. Read the question silently. Now read the three choices. Select the choice that answers the question. Fill in the answer circle.

Put your finger on number 8. Read the question silently. Now read the three choices. Select the choice that answers the question. Fill in the answer circle.

Now we will stop.

Answer Key

1. A
2. C
3. C
4. B
5. C
6. A
7. B
8. C

1. What can you see in the night sky?

   (A) moon and stars

   (B) sun and moon

   (C) air and moon

2. How is the moon different from Earth?

   (A) The moon is green.

   (B) The moon has dinosaurs.

   (C) The moon has no air.

3. How did the moon get its craters?

   (A) Astronauts made them.

   (B) Hurricanes made them.

   (C) Rocks that crashed into it made them.

4. What are a full moon, a half moon, and a quarter moon called?

   (A) moon pictures

   (B) phases of the moon

   (C) weather on the moon

5. Where is our sun located?

   (A) on the moon

   (B) on Earth

   (C) in the center of our solar system

6. Earth moves around the sun in a(n) _____.

   (A) orbit

   (B) circle

   (C) ring

7. Saturn and Mars are called what?

   (A) moons

   (B) planets

   (C) stars

8. How does a telescope help people study space?

   (A) It makes things look smaller.

   (B) It makes things look nicer.

   (C) It makes things look larger.

STOP

Reproduce and pass out page 104 to students.

Teacher Script

Now we are going to answer some questions about fossils. You will read each question silently and then fill in the answer. I will not stop to discuss the questions, but I will go slowly enough for you to finish each one. When you are finished, put your pencil down and sit quietly. Now let's begin.

Put your finger on number 1. Read the question silently. Now read the three choices. Select the choice that answers the question. Fill in the answer circle.

Put your finger on number 2. Read the question silently. Now read the three choices. Select the choice that answers the question. Fill in the answer circle.

Put your finger on number 3. Read the question silently. Now read the three choices. Select the choice that answers the question. Fill in the answer circle.

Put your finger on number 4. Read the question silently. Now read the three choices. Select the choice that answers the question. Fill in the answer circle.

Put your finger on number 5. Read the question silently. Now read the three choices. Select the choice that answers the question. Fill in the answer circle.

Put your finger on number 6. Here there is a blank that you must fill in. Read the sentence silently. Now read the three choices. Select the choice that best completes the sentence. Fill in the answer circle.

Put your finger on number 7. Read the question silently. Now read the three choices. Select the choice that answers the question. Fill in the answer circle.

Put your finger on number 8. Read the question silently. Now read the three choices. Select the choice that answers the question. Fill in the answer circle.

Now we will stop.

Answer Key

1. A
2. C
3. A
4. C
5. B
6. C
7. B
8. A

1. Where would you find a fossil?

    (A) in the ground

    (B) in the sky

    (C) on the moon

2. What is a fossil?

    (A) a type of food for mammals

    (B) a type of rock

    (C) a print of a plant or animal that died a long time ago

3. How do fossils help us learn?

    (A) They can show us what things looked like long ago.

    (B) They can speak to us.

    (C) They can be used to go back in time.

4. If the fossil of an animal has sharp teeth, what did it probably eat when it was alive?

    (A) plants

    (B) fruit

    (C) meat

5. Which one of these has gone extinct?

    (A) alligators

    (B) dinosaurs

    (C) lions

6. If an animal is extinct it means _____.

    (A) it lives only in zoos

    (B) there is not very many of them left

    (C) this type of animal no longer exists

7. What does a paleontologist study?

    (A) fish

    (B) fossils

    (C) dinosaurs

8. How are fossils made?

    (A) Animal and plant parts get buried in mud and rock.

    (B) They are made in factories.

    (C) They are made under the ocean.

STOP

Reproduce and pass out page 106 to students.

Teacher Script

Now we are going to answer some questions about plants. You will read each question silently and then fill in the answer. I will not stop to discuss the questions, but I will go slowly enough for you to finish each one. When you are finished, put your pencil down and sit quietly. Now let's begin.

Put your finger on number 1. Read the question silently. Now read the three choices. Select the choice that answers the question. Fill in the answer circle.

Put your finger on number 2. Read the question silently. Now read the three choices. Select the choice that answers the question. Fill in the answer circle.

Put your finger on number 3. Read the question silently. Now read the three choices. Select the choice that answers the question. Fill in the answer circle.

Put your finger on number 4. Read the question silently. Now read the three choices. Select the choice that answers the question. Fill in the answer circle.

Put your finger on number 5. Read the question silently. Now read the three choices. Select the choice that answers the question. Fill in the answer circle.

Put your finger on number 6. Read the question silently. Now read the three choices. Select the choice that best completes the sentence. Fill in the answer circle.

Put your finger on number 7. Read the question silently. Now read the three choices. Select the choice that answers the question. Fill in the answer circle.

Put your finger on number 8. Read the question silently. Now read the three choices. Select the choice that answers the question. Fill in the answer circle.

Now we will stop.

Answer Key

1. A
2. B
3. C
4. A
5. B
6. B
7. A
8. B

1. What do plants need to grow?

   Ⓐ light

   Ⓑ meat

   Ⓒ vegetables

2. Where would you find the roots of a plant?

   Ⓐ on top of the plant

   Ⓑ in the ground

   Ⓒ on the leaves

3. If plants didn't have roots, what might happen to them?

   Ⓐ They would get really big.

   Ⓑ They would stay really small.

   Ⓒ They would blow away.

4. What part of the plant makes the seeds?

   Ⓐ the flower

   Ⓑ the stem

   Ⓒ the leaves

5. How are seeds scattered from place to place?

   Ⓐ through the mail

   Ⓑ through the air

   Ⓒ in cars

6. What is contained inside of a seed?

   Ⓐ energy

   Ⓑ a tiny plant

   Ⓒ dirt

7. Which of the following comes from a plant?

   Ⓐ bread

   Ⓑ yogurt

   Ⓒ hamburger

8. What is the job of the leaves of a plant?

   Ⓐ to make the seeds

   Ⓑ to make the food

   Ⓒ to hold the plant in place

STOP

Reproduce and pass out page 108 to students.

Teacher Script

Now we are going to answer some questions about animals. You will read each question silently and then fill in the answer. I will not stop to discuss the questions, but I will go slowly enough for you to finish each one. When you are finished, put your pencil down and sit quietly. Now let's begin.

Put your finger on number 1. Read the question silently. Now read the three choices. Select the choice that answers the question. Fill in the answer circle.

Put your finger on number 2. Read the question silently. Now read the three choices. Select the choice that answers the question. Fill in the answer circle.

Put your finger on number 3. Here there is a blank that you must fill in. Read the sentence silently. Now read the three choices. Select the choice that best completes the sentence. Fill in the answer circle.

Put your finger on number 4. Read the question silently. Now read the three choices. Select the choice that answers the question. Fill in the answer circle.

Put your finger on number 5. Here is another blank that you must fill in. Read the sentence silently. Now read the three choices. Select the choice that best completes the sentence. Fill in the answer circle.

Put your finger on number 6. Read the question silently. Now read the three choices. Select the choice that answers the question. Fill in the answer circle.

Put your finger on number 7. Here is another blank. Read the sentence silently. Now read the three choices. Select the choice that best completes the sentence. Fill in the answer circle.

Put your finger on number 8. In this sentence there is a blank. Read the sentence silently. Now read the three choices. Select the choice that best completes the sentence. Fill in the answer circle.

Now we will stop.

Answer Key

1. B
2. C
3. B
4. B
5. A
6. B
7. C
8. A

1. What do most mammals have?

   Ⓐ wings

   Ⓑ fur

   Ⓒ gills

2. Which of the following is a reptile?

   Ⓐ robin

   Ⓑ lion

   Ⓒ snake

3. A tadpole grows up to be a _____.

   Ⓐ butterfly

   Ⓑ frog

   Ⓒ pupa

4. What is a habitat?

   Ⓐ an animal's lifecycle

   Ⓑ where an animal lives

   Ⓒ an endangered animal

5. A whale that eats a seal and a seal that eats smaller fish is an example of _____.

   Ⓐ a food chain

   Ⓑ mammal behavior

   Ⓒ life cycle

6. If an animal's habitat changed, what might happen?

   Ⓐ Nothing would change.

   Ⓑ The animal could become endangered.

   Ⓒ The animal would become happy.

7. An animal changing color is an example of _____.

   Ⓐ life cycle

   Ⓑ food chain

   Ⓒ camouflage

8. The shell of a turtle is used for _____.

   Ⓐ protection

   Ⓑ food

   Ⓒ camouflage

STOP

Earth Science

Reproduce and pass out page 110 to students.

Teacher Script

Now we are going to answer some questions about Earth. You will read each question silently and then fill in the answer. I will not stop to discuss the questions, but I will go slowly enough for you for you to finish each one. When you are finished, put your pencil down and sit quietly. Now let's begin.

Put your finger on number 1. Read the question silently. Now read the three choices. Select the choice that answers the question. Fill in the answer circle.

Put your finger on number 2. Read the question silently. Now read the three choices. Select the choice that answers the question. Fill in the answer circle.

Put your finger on number 3. Read the question silently. Now read the three choices. Select the choice that answers the question. Fill in the answer circle.

Put your finger on number 4. Here there is a blank that you must fill in. Read the sentence silently. Now read the three choices. Select the choice that best completes the sentence. Fill in the answer circle.

Put your finger on number 5. Read the question silently. Now read the three choices. Select the choice that answers the question. Fill in the answer circle.

Put your finger on number 6. Read the question silently. Now read the three choices. Select the choice that answers the question. Fill in the answer circle.

Put your finger on number 7. Read the question silently. Now read the three choices. Select the choice that answers the question. Fill in the answer circle.

Put your finger on number 8. Read the question silently. Now read the three choices. Select the choice that answers the question. Fill in the answer circle.

Now we will stop.

Answer Key

1. A
2. B
3. C
4. B
5. A
6. C
7. A
8. B

1. What is lava?

   Ⓐ molten rock

   Ⓑ small pebbles

   Ⓒ large boulders

2. Where does lava come from?

   Ⓐ from the sky

   Ⓑ from inside of Earth

   Ⓒ from earthquakes

3. What are rocks made of?

   Ⓐ sand

   Ⓑ fossils

   Ⓒ minerals

4. A flowing river wearing away the land is an example of _____.

   Ⓐ earthquakes

   Ⓑ erosion

   Ⓒ lava flow

5. Which one is a natural resource?

   Ⓐ water

   Ⓑ plastic

   Ⓒ paper

6. What comes out of a volcano?

   Ⓐ rocks

   Ⓑ minerals

   Ⓒ lava

7. Why is it important to recycle?

   Ⓐ Recycling makes less waste.

   Ⓑ People will think you are smart.

   Ⓒ It's easy to do.

8. Where do small rocks come from?

   Ⓐ from the ocean

   Ⓑ from the bigger rocks

   Ⓒ from the store

STOP

Reproduce and pass out page 112 to students.

Teacher Script

Now we are going to answer some questions about the weather. I will ask you a question about each row, and you will fill in the answer. I will not stop to discuss the questions, but I will go slowly enough for you for you to finish each one. When you are finished, put your pencil down and sit quietly. Now let's begin.

Put your finger on number 1. Read the question silently. Now read the three choices. Select the choice that answers the question. Fill in the answer circle.

Put your finger on number 2. Read the question silently. Now read the three choices. Select the choice that answers the question. Fill in the answer circle.

Put your finger on number 3. Read the question silently. Now read the three choices. Select the choice that answers the question. Fill in the answer circle.

Put your finger on number 4. Read the question silently. Now read the three choices. Select the choice that answers the question. Fill in the answer circle.

Put your finger on number 5. Read the question silently. Now read the three choices. Select the choice that answers the question. Fill in the answer circle.

Put your finger on number 6. Read the question silently. Now read the three choices. Select the choice that best completes the sentence. Fill in the answer circle.

Put your finger on number 7. Read the question silently. Look carefully at the three pictures. Select the choice that answers the question. Fill in the answer circle.

Put your finger on number 8. Read the question silently. Now read the three choices. Select the choice that answers the question. Fill in the answer circle.

Now we will stop.

Answer Key

1. B
2. B
3. C
4. B
5. C
6. A
7. A
8. B

1. What does this measure?

- (A) the speed of the wind
- (B) the temperature of the air
- (C) the distance of the sun

2. Which season is usually the hottest?

- (A) spring
- (B) summer
- (C) autumn

3. Which season is usually the rainiest?

- (A) summer
- (B) winter
- (C) spring

4. In what season do some animals hibernate?

- (A) autumn
- (B) winter
- (C) spring

5. What happens when water evaporates?

- (A) It disappears.
- (B) It condenses.
- (C) It becomes a gas.

6. What happens when water vapor condenses?

- (A) It becomes a liquid.
- (B) Clouds turn gray.
- (C) It snows.

7. Where should you never stand during a thunderstorm?

(A)  (B)  (C)

8. What is the opposite of a flood?

- (A) tornado
- (B) drought
- (C) hurricane

Motion, Magnets, and Electricity

Reproduce and pass out page 114 to students.

Teacher Script

Now we are going to answer some questions about motion, magnets, and electricity. You will read each question silently and then fill in the answer. I will not stop to discuss the questions, but I will go slowly enough for you for you to finish each one. When you are finished, put your pencil down and sit quietly. Now let's begin.

Put your finger on number 1. Read the question silently. Look carefully at the picture. Now read the three choices. Select the choice that answers the question. Fill in the answer circle.

Put your finger on number 2. Read the question silently. Look carefully at the picture. Now read the three choices. Select the choice that answers the question. Fill in the answer circle.

Put your finger on number 3. Read the question silently. Now read the three choices. Select the choice that answers the question. Fill in the answer circle.

Put your finger on number 4. Read the question silently. Now read the three choices. Select the choice that answers the question. Fill in the answer circle.

Put your finger on number 5. Read the question silently. Now read the three choices. Select the choice that answers the question. Fill in the answer circle.

Put your finger on number 6. Read the question silently. Look carefully at the pictures. Now read the three choices. Select the choice that answers the question. Fill in the answer circle.

Put your finger on number 7. Read the question silently. Look carefully at the pictures. Now read the three choices. Select the choice that answers the question. Fill in the answer circle.

Put your finger on number 8. Read the question silently. Now read the three choices. Select the choice that answers the question. Fill in the answer circle.

Now we will stop.

Answer Key

1. B
2. C
3. B
4. C
5. B
6. A
7. A
8. B

Motion, Magnets, and Electricity

1. Which force is being used to move this wagon?

Ⓐ push
Ⓑ pull
Ⓒ friction

2. Which force is being used to move this bike?

Ⓐ gravity
Ⓑ pull
Ⓒ push

3. Which force causes a ball to fall to the ground?

Ⓐ push
Ⓑ gravity
Ⓒ magnetism

4. Where are a magnet's poles?

Ⓐ in the middle
Ⓑ on the front
Ⓒ at the ends

5. If you put the north poles of two magnets together, what would happen?

Ⓐ They would attract each other.
Ⓑ They would repel each other.
Ⓒ They would produce an electric shock.

6. Which object could a magnet attract?

Ⓐ   Ⓑ   Ⓒ

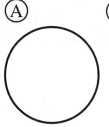 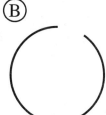 

7. Which of these best shows how electricity travels?

Ⓐ   Ⓑ   Ⓒ

8. What is the path that electricity travels called?

Ⓐ a battery
Ⓑ a circuit
Ⓒ stored energy

Reproduce and pass out page 116 to students.

Teacher Script

Now we are going to answer some questions about matter. You will read each question silently and then fill in the answer. I will not stop to discuss the questions, but I will go slowly enough for you for you to finish each one. When you are finished, put your pencil down and sit quietly. Now let's begin.

Put your finger on number 1. Read the question silently. Now read the three choices. Select the choice that answers the question. Fill in the answer circle.

Put your finger on number 2. Read the question silently. Now read the three choices. Select the choice that answers the question. Fill in the answer circle.

Put your finger on number 3. Read the question silently. Now read the three choices. Select the choice that answers the question. Fill in the answer circle.

Put your finger on number 4. Read the question silently. Now read the three choices. Select the choice that answers the question. Fill in the answer circle.

Put your finger on number 5. Read the question silently. Now read the three choices. Select the choice that answers the question. Fill in the answer circle.

Put your finger on number 6. Here there is a blank that you must fill in. Read the sentence silently. Now read the three choices. Select the choice that best completes the sentence. Fill in the answer circle.

Put your finger on number 7. Read the question silently. Now read the three choices. Select the choice that answers the question. Fill in the answer circle.

Put your finger on number 8. Read the question silently. Now read the three choices. Select the choice that answers the question. Fill in the answer circle.

Now we will stop.

Answer Key

1. A
2. B
3. B
4. A
5. C
6. C
7. C
8. A

1. Which of these is a state of matter?

   (A) solid

   (B) rock

   (C) gravity

2. Which of these is an example of matter?

   (A) gravity

   (B) air

   (C) electricity

3. In which state of matter is water?

   (A) gas

   (B) liquid

   (C) solid

4. What can change the state of matter?

   (A) heat

   (B) friction

   (C) gravity

5. If you pour soup into a bowl what shape does it take?

   (A) a square shape

   (B) a round shape

   (C) a bowl shape

6. If water is frozen it has been changed _____.

   (A) from a gas into a solid

   (B) from a liquid into a gas

   (C) from a liquid into a solid

7. A hot dog in a bun is an example of what?

   (A) two liquids mixed together

   (B) two gases mixed together

   (C) two solids mixed together

8. Meatballs and sauce are an example of what?

   (A) a solid and a liquid mixed together

   (B) a solid and a gas mixed together

   (C) two gases mixed together

STOP

Heat, Sound, and Light

Reproduce and pass out page 118 to students.

Teacher Script

Now we are going to answer some questions about heat, sound, and light. You will read each question silently and then fill in the answer. I will not stop to discuss the questions, but I will go slowly enough for you for you to finish each one. When you are finished, put your pencil down and sit quietly. Now let's begin.

Put your finger on number 1. Read the question silently. Now read the three choices. Select the choice that answers the question. Fill in the answer circle.

Put your finger on number 2. Here is a blank that you must fill in. Read the sentence silently. Now read the three choices. Select the choice that best completes the sentence. Fill in the answer circle.

Put your finger on number 3. Here's another blank. Read the sentence silently. Now read the three choices. Select the choice that best completes the sentence. Fill in the answer circle.

Put your finger on number 4. Read the question silently. Now read the three choices. Select the choice that answers the question. Fill in the answer circle.

Put your finger on number 5. Read the question silently. Now read the three choices. Select the choice that answers the question. Fill in the answer circle.

Put your finger on number 6. Read the question silently. Now read the three choices. Select the choice that answers the question. Fill in the answer circle.

Put your finger on number 7. Read the question silently. Look carefully at the three choices. Select the choice that answers the question. Fill in the answer circle.

Put your finger on number 8. Read the question silently. Now read the three choices. Select the choice that answers the question. Fill in the answer circle.

Now we will stop.

Answer Key

1. C
2. A
3. B
4. A
5. B
6. C
7. B
8. C

Heat, Sound, and Light

1. When an object vibrates, what is created?

   Ⓐ attraction

   Ⓑ gravity

   Ⓒ sound

2. If a sound has a high volume it means that it is _____.

   Ⓐ loud

   Ⓑ soft

   Ⓒ high-pitched

3. A tuba has a pitch that is _____.

   Ⓐ high

   Ⓑ low

   Ⓒ soft

4. Which one is a source of heat?

   Ⓐ sun

   Ⓑ moon

   Ⓒ sink

5. What are the colors of a rainbow?

   Ⓐ red, tan, orange, yellow, blue, violet

   Ⓑ red, orange, yellow, green, blue, indigo, violet

   Ⓒ pink, red, green, black, blue, orange, violet

6. Which two things make a rainbow?

   Ⓐ heat and water

   Ⓑ heat and wind

   Ⓒ light and water

7. Which one shows how light travels?

   Ⓐ

   Ⓑ

   Ⓒ

8. Which one can light pass through?

   Ⓐ brick wall

   Ⓑ black window shade

   Ⓒ cup of water

STOP

Reproduce and pass out page 120 to students.

Teacher Script

Now we are going to answer some questions about our bodies. You will read each question silently and then fill in the answer. I will not stop to discuss the questions, but I will go slowly enough for you for you to finish each one. When you are finished, put your pencil down and sit quietly. Now let's begin.

Put your finger on number 1. Read the question silently. Now read the three choices. Select the choice that answers the question. Fill in the answer circle.

Put your finger on number 2. Read the question silently. Now read the three choices. Select the choice that answers the question. Fill in the answer circle.

Put your finger on number 3. Read the question silently. Now read the three choices. Select the choice that answers the question. Fill in the answer circle.

Put your finger on number 4. Read the question silently. Now read the three choices. Select the choice that answers the question. Fill in the answer circle.

Put your finger on number 5. Read the question silently. Now read the three choices. Select the choice that answers the question. Fill in the answer circle.

Put your finger on number 6. Read the question silently. Now read the three choices. Select the choice that answers the question. Fill in the answer circle.

Put your finger on number 7. Read the question silently. Now read the three choices. Select the choice that answers the question. Fill in the answer circle.

Put your finger on number 8. Read the question silently. Now read the three choices. Select the choice that answers the question. Fill in the answer circle.

Now we will stop.

Answer Key

1. A
2. A
3. C
4. A
5. B
6. B
7. A
8. B

Human Body

1. Where is your brain located?
   - (A) head
   - (B) chest
   - (C) belly

2. What does your brain use to send messages to your body?
   - (A) nerves
   - (B) blood
   - (C) oxygen

3. What helps to protect your brain?
   - (A) muscle
   - (B) skin
   - (C) skull

4. What is the job of your heart?
   - (A) to pump blood
   - (B) digest food
   - (C) to help us breathe

5. What does your blood travel through?
   - (A) nerves
   - (B) veins
   - (C) skin

6. Where does the food you eat go after it leaves the stomach?
   - (A) to the esophagus
   - (B) to the intestines
   - (C) to the brain

7. Where does digestion begin?
   - (A) the mouth
   - (B) the stomach
   - (C) the large intestine

8. Which part of the body helps us breathe?
   - (A) the stomach
   - (B) the lungs
   - (C) the heart

STOP

Reproduce and pass out pages 122 to students.

Teacher Script

Now we are going to answer some questions about Earth's features. You will read each question silently and then fill in the answer. I will not stop to discuss the questions, but I will go slowly enough for you to finish each one. When you are finished, put your pencil down and sit quietly. Now let's begin.

Put your finger on number 1. Read the question silently. Now read the three choices. Select the choice that answers the question. Fill in the answer circle.

Put your finger on number 2. Here there is a blank that you must fill in. Read the sentence silently. Now read the three choices. Select the choice that best completes the sentence. Fill in the answer circle.

Put your finger on number 3. Read the question silently. Now read the three choices. Select the choice that answers the question. Fill in the answer circle.

Put your finger on number 4. Read the question silently. Now read the three choices. Select the choice that answers the question. Fill in the answer circle.

Put your finger on number 5. Read the question silently. Now read the three choices. Select the choice that answers the question. Fill in the answer circle.

Put your finger on number 6. Here you must fill in the blank again. Read the sentence silently. Now read the three choices. Select the choice that best completes the sentence. Fill in the answer circle.

Put your finger on number 7. Here is another blank. Read the sentence silently. Now read the three choices. Select the choice that best completes the sentence. Fill in the answer circle.

Put your finger on number 8. Read the question silently. Now read the three choices. Select the choice that answers the question. Fill in the answer circle.

Now we will stop.

Answer Key

1. B
2. C
3. A
4. C
5. B
6. A
7. C
8. B

1. Which type of landform could you climb?

Ⓐ island

Ⓑ mountain

Ⓒ peninsula

2. An island is _____.

Ⓐ land between mountains

Ⓑ the same as a shoreline

Ⓒ land completely surrounded by water

3. Low-lying land is also called what?

Ⓐ a valley

Ⓑ a peninsula

Ⓒ a peak

4. What is a lake surrounded by?

Ⓐ an ocean

Ⓑ mountains

Ⓒ land

5. Which body of water usually contains salt?

Ⓐ river

Ⓑ ocean

Ⓒ stream

6. A plain is an area of _____.

Ⓐ flat land

Ⓑ hilly land

Ⓒ fertile land

7. A piece of land almost surrounded by water is called a(n) _____.

Ⓐ island

Ⓑ isthmus

Ⓒ peninsula

8. Which sentence is true?

Ⓐ Oceans are made up of fresh water.

Ⓑ Rivers flow into oceans.

Ⓒ Lakes flow into oceans.

STOP

Map Skills

Reproduce and pass out pages 124 and 125 to students.

Teacher Script

Now we are going to look at a map and answer questions about it. When you answer these kinds of questions, it's important to look carefully at the map to find the answers to the questions you are being asked. You will read each question silently and then fill in the answer. I will not stop to discuss the questions, but I will go slowly enough for you for you to finish each one. When you are finished, put your pencil down and sit quietly. Now let's begin.

Put your finger on number 1. Read the question silently. Now read the three choices. Look at the map and select the choice that answers the question. Fill in the answer circle.

Put your finger on number 2. Read the question silently. Now read the three choices. Look at the map and select the choice that answers the question. Fill in the answer circle.

Put your finger on number 3. Read the question silently. Now read the three choices. Look at the map and select the choice that answers the question. Fill in the answer circle.

Put your finger on number 4. Here is a blank that you must fill in. Read the sentence silently. Now read the three choices. Look at the map and select the choice that best completes the sentence. Fill in the answer circle.

Put your finger on number 5. Read the question silently. Now read the three choices. Look at the map and select the choice that answers the question. Fill in the answer circle.

Put your finger on number 6. Read the question silently. Now read the three choices. Look at the map and select the choice that answers the question. Fill in the answer circle.

Put your finger on number 7. Here is another blank. Read the sentence silently. Now read the three choices. Look at the map and select the choice that best completes the sentence. Fill in the answer circle.

Put your finger on number 8. Notice the blank? Read the sentence silently. Now read the three choices. Look at the map and select the choice that best completes the sentence. Fill in the answer circle.

Now we will stop.

Answer Key

1. B
2. B
3. B
4. A
5. A
6. C
7. B
8. C

Shoe Town

Pet Central

Gifts Galore

Stars Drive

Grocery Store

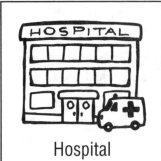
Hospital

Tina's Flowers

Blue Street

Moon Street

Pink Avenue

Bus Stop

Kidz Clothes

Bakery

Sun Avenue

Library

School

Park

Map Skills

1. What is this a map of?
   (A) a shopping mall
   (B) a city
   (C) a carnival

2. Where is the grocery store located?
   (A) next to the school
   (B) across from the hospital
   (C) on Pink Avenue

3. In which direction would you have to walk to get from the park to the bakery?
   (A) south
   (B) north
   (C) west

4. Sun Avenue is _____ of Moon Street.
   (A) south
   (B) east
   (C) north

5. Which place is located near the corner of Blue Street and Moon Street?
   (A) Kidz Clothes
   (B) Shoe Town
   (C) Tina's Flowers

6. Between which two streets is the hospital located?
   (A) Blue Street and Sun Avenue
   (B) Moon Street and Sun Avenue
   (C) Moon Street and Stars Drive

7. Tina's Flowers is located _____ of Gifts Galore.
   (A) north
   (B) south
   (C) west

8. The library is located _____ of the school.
   (A) east
   (B) south
   (C) west

STOP

Government

Reproduce and pass out page 127 to students.

Teacher Script

Now we are going to answer some questions about our government. You will read each question silently and then fill in the answer. I will not stop to discuss the questions, but I will go slowly enough for you for you to finish each one. When you are finished, put your pencil down and sit quietly.

Put your finger on number 1. Read the question silently. Now read the three choices. Select the choice that answers the question. Fill in the answer circle.

Put your finger on number 2. Read the question silently. Now read the three choices. Select the choice that answers the question. Fill in the answer circle.

Put your finger on number 3. Read the question silently. Now read the three choices. Select the choice that answers the question. Fill in the answer circle.

Put your finger on number 4. Here is a blank that you must fill in. Read the sentence silently. Now read the three choices. Select the choice that best completes the sentence. Fill in the answer circle.

Put your finger on number 5. Read the question silently. Now read the three choices. Select the choice that answers the question. Fill in the answer circle.

Put your finger on number 6. Here is another blank that must be filled in. Read the sentence silently. Now read the three choices. Select the choice that best completes the sentence. Fill in the answer circle.

Put your finger on number 7. Read the question silently. Now read the three choices. Select the choice that answers the question. Fill in the answer circle.

Put your finger on number 8. Read the question silently. Now read the three choices. Select the choice that answers the question. Fill in the answer circle.

Now we will stop.

Answer Key

1. C
2. C
3. C
4. B
5. A
6. A
7. A
8. C

1. What is the job of a mayor?

Ⓐ A mayor leads a state.

Ⓑ A mayor leads a country.

Ⓒ A mayor leads a city.

2. What do governments do for people?

Ⓐ They help keep people safe.

Ⓑ They pay for community services.

Ⓒ Both of these.

3. What are citizens?

Ⓐ elected officials

Ⓑ police

Ⓒ The people who live in a certain area.

4. The person who leads a state is the _____.

Ⓐ senator

Ⓑ governor

Ⓒ mayor

5. What is the capitol of the United States of America?

Ⓐ Washington, D.C.

Ⓑ Philadelphia, Pennsylvania

Ⓒ New York, New York

6. The leader of the United States is called the _____.

Ⓐ president

Ⓑ chief

Ⓒ judge

7. Who are part of the Supreme Court?

Ⓐ judges

Ⓑ doctors

Ⓒ governors

8. How do mayors, governors, and presidents get their jobs?

Ⓐ They are appointed.

Ⓑ They have to be police first.

Ⓒ They are elected by citizens.

STOP

Reproduce and pass out page 129 to students.

Teacher Script

Now we are going to answer some questions about our country. You will read each question silently and then fill in the answer. I will not stop to discuss the questions, but I will go slowly enough for you for you to finish each one. When you are finished, put your pencil down and sit quietly.

Put your finger on number 1. Read the question silently. Now read the three choices. Select the choice that answers the question. Fill in the answer circle.

Put your finger on number 2. Read the question silently. Now read the three choices. Select the choice that answers the question. Fill in the answer circle.

Put your finger on number 3. Read the question silently. Now read the three choices. Select the choice that answers the question. Fill in the answer circle.

Put your finger on number 4. Here is a blank that you must fill in. Read the sentence silently. Now read the three choices. Select the choice that best completes the sentence. Fill in the answer circle.

Put your finger on number 5. Read the question silently. Now read the three choices. Select the choice that answers the question. Fill in the answer circle.

Put your finger on number 6. Read the question silently. Now read the three choices. Select the choice that answers the question. Fill in the answer circle.

Put your finger on number 7. Read the question silently. Now read the three choices. Select the choice that answers the question. Fill in the answer circle.

Put your finger on number 8. Read the question silently. Now read the three choices. Select the choice that answers the question. Fill in the answer circle.

Now we will stop.

Answer Key

1. B
2. A
3. B
4. B
5. A
6. B
7. C
8. B

1. Where is the Statue of Liberty located?

   Ⓐ in Washington, D.C.

   Ⓑ in New York Harbor

   Ⓒ in Hollywood, California

2. On which day do we celebrate our independence?

   Ⓐ July 4th

   Ⓑ October 31st

   Ⓒ the last Thursday in November

3. In what month do we celebrate Martin Luther King, Jr. Day?

   Ⓐ February

   Ⓑ January

   Ⓒ December

4. A national landmark is _____.

   Ⓐ an important date

   Ⓑ an important place

   Ⓒ an important law

5. What is an immigrant?

   Ⓐ a person who goes to live in a new country

   Ⓑ a person from China

   Ⓒ a citizen of the United States

6. Who do we honor on Veterans Day?

   Ⓐ presidents

   Ⓑ soldiers

   Ⓒ pilgrims

7. What does the Statue of Liberty stand for?

   Ⓐ the environment

   Ⓑ citizens

   Ⓒ freedom

8. What is a custom?

   Ⓐ a type of building

   Ⓑ the food, music, and clothing of a certain group

   Ⓒ a type of school

STOP

Reproduce and pass out page 131 to students.

Teacher Script

Now we are going to answer some questions about different kinds of communities. You will read each question silently and then fill in the answer. I will not stop to discuss the questions, but I will go slowly enough for you for you to finish each one. When you are finished, put your pencil down and sit quietly.

Put your finger on number 1. Read the question silently. Now read the three choices. Select the choice that answers the question. Fill in the answer circle.

Put your finger on number 2. Read the question silently. Now read the three choices. Select the choice that answers the question. Fill in the answer circle.

Put your finger on number 3. Here is a blank that you must fill in. Read the sentence silently. Now read the three choices. Select the choice that best completes the sentence. Fill in the answer circle.

Put your finger on number 4. Here's another blank. Read the sentence silently. Now read the three choices. Select the choice that best completes the sentence. Fill in the answer circle.

Put your finger on number 5. Read the question silently. Now read the three choices. Select the choice that answers the question. Fill in the answer circle.

Put your finger on number 6. Read the question silently. Now read the three choices. Select the choice that answers the question. Fill in the answer circle.

Put your finger on number 7. Read the question silently. Now read the three choices. Select the choice that answers the question. Fill in the answer circle.

Put your finger on number 8. Read the question silently. Now read the three choices. Select the choice that answers the question. Fill in the answer circle.

Now we will stop.

Answer Key

1. A
2. B
3. C
4. B
5. C
6. A
7. A
8. B

1. Why are rules important?

Ⓐ They keep us safe.

Ⓑ They keep us happy.

Ⓒ They make us smart.

2. What are the rules of a community called?

Ⓐ crimes

Ⓑ laws

Ⓒ community rules

3. An urban community is the same as _____.

Ⓐ a farm

Ⓑ the suburbs

Ⓒ a city

4. Suburbs are near _____.

Ⓐ farms

Ⓑ cities

Ⓒ small towns

5. Which type of community has the fewest people?

Ⓐ an urban community

Ⓑ a suburban community

Ⓒ a rural community

6. If people want to change a law in their community, what can they do?

Ⓐ vote

Ⓑ nothing

Ⓒ fight

7. Which one is the largest?

Ⓐ a state

Ⓑ a neighborhood

Ⓒ a city

8. If people didn't obey the laws in their community, what might happen?

Ⓐ People would get angry.

Ⓑ People would get hurt.

Ⓒ Nothing would happen.

STOP

Reproduce and pass out page 133 to students.

Teacher Script

Now we are going to answer some questions about geography. You will read each question silently and then fill in the answer. I will not stop to discuss the questions, but I will go slowly enough for you for you to finish each one. When you are finished, put your pencil down and sit quietly.

Put your finger on number 1. Read the question silently. Now read the three choices. Select the choice that answers the question. Fill in the answer circle.

Put your finger on number 2. Read the question silently. Now read the three choices. Select the choice that answers the question. Fill in the answer circle.

Put your finger on number 3. Read the question silently. Now read the three choices. Select the choice that answers the question. Fill in the answer circle.

Put your finger on number 4. Read the question silently. Now read the three choices. Select the choice that answers the question. Fill in the answer circle.

Put your finger on number 5. Read the question silently. Now read the three choices. Select the choice that answers the question. Fill in the answer circle.

Put your finger on number 6. Read the question silently. Now read the three choices. Select the choice that answers the question. Fill in the answer circle.

Put your finger on number 7. Read the question silently. Now read the three choices. Select the choice that answers the question. Fill in the answer circle.

Put your finger on number 8. Read the question silently. Now read the three choices. Select the choice that answers the question. Fill in the answer circle.

Now we will stop.

Answer Key

1. A
2. C
3. B
4. C
5. A
6. B
7. C
8. B

Geography

1. Which two countries border the United States?

   Ⓐ Mexico and Canada

   Ⓑ England and France

   Ⓒ Puerto Rico and Mexico

2. On what continent do you live?

   Ⓐ South America

   Ⓑ The United States of America

   Ⓒ North America

3. How many continents are there?

   Ⓐ 5

   Ⓑ 7

   Ⓒ 10

4. Which oceans border the United States?

   Ⓐ Pacific and Indian

   Ⓑ Pacific and Arctic

   Ⓒ Pacific and Atlantic

5. How many oceans are there on Earth?

   Ⓐ 5

   Ⓑ 3

   Ⓒ 7

6. Why is a globe a good model of Earth?

   Ⓐ because it is a different shape than Earth

   Ⓑ because it is the same shape as Earth

   Ⓒ because it is flat like Earth

7. What is the equator?

   Ⓐ the name of a country

   Ⓑ the name of a city

   Ⓒ an imaginary line that divides Earth in half

8. What is a continent?

   Ⓐ a large body of water

   Ⓑ a large piece of land

   Ⓒ a large island

Reproduce and pass out page 135 to students.

Teacher Script

Now we are going to answer some questions about the history of our country. You will read each question silently and then fill in the answer. I will not stop to discuss the questions, but I will go slowly enough for you for you to finish each one. When you are finished, put your pencil down and sit quietly.

Put your finger on number 1. Read the question silently. Now read the three choices. Select the choice that answers the question. Fill in the answer circle.

Put your finger on number 2. Read the question silently. Now read the three choices. Select the choice that answers the question. Fill in the answer circle.

Put your finger on number 3. Read the question silently. Now read the three choices. Select the choice that answers the question. Fill in the answer circle.

Put your finger on number 4. Read the question silently. Now read the three choices. Select the choice that answers the question. Fill in the answer circle.

Put your finger on number 5. Read the question silently. Now read the three choices. Select the choice that answers the question. Fill in the answer circle.

Put your finger on number 6. Read the question silently. Now read the three choices. Select the choice that answers the question. Fill in the answer circle.

Put your finger on number 7. Read the question silently. Now read the three choices. Select the choice that answers the question. Fill in the answer circle.

Put your finger on number 8. Read the question silently. Now read the three choices. Select the choice that answers the question. Fill in the answer circle.

Now we will stop.

Answer Key

1. A
2. B
3. A
4. C
5. C
6. A
7. B
8. C

1. Who were the first people to live in North America?

Ⓐ Native Americans

Ⓑ African Americans

Ⓒ British Americans

2. Sioux and Pueblo are the names of what?

Ⓐ types of Native American food

Ⓑ names of Native American tribes

Ⓒ names of Native American songs

3. What kinds of shelters did some early Native Americans live in?

Ⓐ tepees

Ⓑ condos

Ⓒ forts

4. What was Jamestown?

Ⓐ a Native American community

Ⓑ an early American city

Ⓒ an early English colony

5. Who was John Smith?

Ⓐ the first president of the United States

Ⓑ the first explorer to North America

Ⓒ the leader of the Jamestown colony

6. What was the *Mayflower*?

Ⓐ the name of the pilgrim's ship

Ⓑ the name of a colony

Ⓒ the name of a Native American tribe

7. Why were the Native Americans so important to the pilgrims?

Ⓐ They taught them how to dance and sing.

Ⓑ They showed them how to get food.

Ⓒ They taught them how to read and write.

8. On which holiday do we honor the help of the Native Americans?

Ⓐ Christmas

Ⓑ Memorial Day

Ⓒ Thanksgiving

Reproduce and pass out page 137 to students.

Teacher Script

Now we are going to answer some questions about the history of our country. You will read each question silently and then fill in the answer. I will not stop to discuss the questions, but I will go slowly enough for you for you to finish each one. When you are finished, put your pencil down and sit quietly.

Put your finger on number 1. Read the question silently. Now read the three choices. Select the choice that answers the question. Fill in the answer circle.

Put your finger on number 2. Read the question silently. Now read the three choices. Select the choice that answers the question. Fill in the answer circle.

Put your finger on number 3. Read the question silently. Now read the three choices. Select the choice that answers the question. Fill in the answer circle.

Put your finger on number 4. Read the question silently. Now read the three choices. Select the choice that answers the question. Fill in the answer circle.

Put your finger on number 5. Read the question silently. Now read the three choices. Select the choice that answers the question. Fill in the answer circle.

Put your finger on number 6. Read the question silently. Now read the three choices. Select the choice that answers the question. Fill in the answer circle.

Put your finger on number 7. Read the question silently. Now read the three choices. Select the choice that answers the question. Fill in the answer circle.

Put your finger on number 8. Read the question silently. Now read the three choices. Select the choice that answers the question. Fill in the answer circle.

Now we will stop.

Answer Key

1. A
2. B
3. C
4. B
5. B
6. B
7. C
8. A

1. How many original colonies were there in America?

(A) 13

(B) 10

(C) 50

2. Where were the colonies located?

(A) on the west coast of America

(B) on the east coast of America

(C) on the east and west coasts of America

3. What did the colonists want from England?

(A) money

(B) taxes

(C) independence

4. Who lead the colonial army?

(A) Thomas Jefferson

(B) George Washington

(C) Patrick Henry

5. Who were Lewis and Clark?

(A) presidents

(B) explorers

(C) kings

6. What part of the country did Lewis and Clark explore?

(A) the east

(B) the west

(C) the north

7. What kind of transportation did the pioneers use?

(A) cars

(B) trains

(C) covered wagons

8. What war ended slavery?

(A) Civil War

(B) War for Independence

(C) The French-Indian War

Reproduce and pass out page 139 to students.

Teacher Script

Now we are going to answer some questions about resources. You will read each question silently and then fill in the answer. I will not stop to discuss the questions, but I will go slowly enough for you for you to finish each one. When you are finished, put your pencil down and sit quietly.

Put your finger on number 1. Here there is a blank that you must fill in. Read the sentence silently. Now read the three choices. Select the choice that best completes the sentence. Fill in the answer circle.

Put your finger on number 2. Here is another blank. Read the sentence silently. Now read the three choices. Select the choice that best completes the sentence. Fill in the answer circle.

Put your finger on number 3. Here is another blank. Read the sentence silently. Now read the three choices. Select the choice that best completes the sentence. Fill in the answer circle.

Put your finger on number 4. Read the question silently. Now read the three choices. Select the choice that answers the question. Fill in the answer circle.

Put your finger on number 5. Here is another blank. Read the sentence silently. Now read the three choices. Select the choice that best completes the sentence. Fill in the answer circle.

Put your finger on number 6. Here's another blank. Read the sentence silently. Now read the three choices. Select the choice that best completes the sentence. Fill in the answer circle.

Put your finger on number 7. Read the question silently. Now read the three choices. Select the choice that answers the question. Fill in the answer circle.

Put your finger on number 8. Here's another blank. Read the sentence silently. Now read the three choices. Select the choice that best completes the sentence. Fill in the answer circle.

Now we will stop.

Answer Key

1. B
2. B
3. C
4. C
5. C
6. B
7. C
8. A

1. Another name for a farmer is
   _____.
   - (A) a consumer
   - (B) a producer
   - (C) a doctor

2. If you buy a gallon of milk it means that you are _____.
   - (A) a producer
   - (B) a consumer
   - (C) a farmer

3. Something that comes from the Earth that people use is called _____.
   - (A) a resource
   - (B) a product
   - (C) a natural resource

4. Which one is not a natural resource?
   - (A) water
   - (B) trees
   - (C) plastic

5. A crop is _____.
   - (A) a type of tree
   - (B) a type of fruit
   - (C) a type of plant that farmers grow

6. The money people earn from their jobs is called _____.
   - (A) cash
   - (B) income
   - (C) goods

7. Which one of these people provides a service?
   - (A) brother
   - (B) student
   - (C) teacher

8. Transportation means _____.
   - (A) moving people and goods from place to place
   - (B) trading food
   - (C) paying taxes

STOP

Parent Handout: Reading

Tips for Parents: Help Your Child with Reading

You are your child's first teacher. According to the National Institute of Education, the most important thing you can do to help your child succeed in school is to read aloud to him or her. Reading to your child makes him or her feel respected and part of your world. It builds self-esteem.

Reading aloud to your child stimulates the mind, strengthens the imagination, and makes your child curious about the world. Reading aloud will help your child to understand words, master language, and enable him or her to arrive at school feeling confident.

How You Can Help

1. **Make the reading time special.** Turn off the TV, radio, or anything that will distract from your time together. Story time can be a special part of every day—before bedtime or after a nap. Be responsive at other times, too, if your child brings a book and needs quiet time with you.

2. **Patience!** Reading to children takes time, but you will be letting them know how important they are to you. Children also love to read favorite books over and over again. Being comfortable with a book gives them confidence.

3. **Have your child choose the book you will be reading together.** Sit close together. Hold the book so your child can see it, and let him or her turn the pages.

4. **Take time to look at the pictures and talk about them.** Ask your child what he or she thinks is happening or what the characters are feeling.

5. **Make the story come to life by reading with expression.** Change your voice to become different characters or to fit different situations (deep/low, quiet/soft). Ask your child to make special sounds with you—a growling animal or a howling wind.

6. **Stop at interesting points in the story and ask questions** such as "What do you think will happen next?" or "What would you do if you were there?" Help your child relate the story to his or her own experiences by asking questions like "Have you ever felt that way?" Listening to what your child has to say lets him or her know that his or her thoughts are important to you.

7. **Have fun with books and language.** Play games, sing songs, and create rhymes with your children. Read books that offer funny situations and characters so you can enjoy them and laugh together.

8. **Finally, the library can be a familiar and special place for you and your child.** Obtain a library card in your child's name. This will build self-esteem and give him or her a sense of involvement.

Tips for Parents: Help Your Child with Math

It is highly likely that when you studied math, you were expected to complete lots of problems accurately and quickly. There was only one way to arrive at your answers, and it was believed that the best way to improve math ability was to do more problems and to do them fast. Today, the focus is less on the quantity of memorized problems and more on understanding the concepts and applying thinking skills to arrive at an answer. While accuracy is always important, a wrong answer may help you and your child discover what your child may not understand. You might find some of the following thoughts helpful when thinking about wrong answers:

➤ **Realize problems can be solved in different ways.** While problems in math may have only one solution, there may be many ways to get the right answer. When working on math problems with your child, ask, "Could you tell me how you got that answer?" Your child's way might be different from yours. If the answer is correct and the strategy or way of solving it has worked, it is a great alternative. By encouraging children to talk about what they are thinking, we help them to become stronger mathematicians and independent thinkers.

➤ **Realize doing math in your head is important.** Have you ever noticed that today very few people take their pencil and paper out to solve problems in the grocery, fast food, or department store or in the office? Instead, most people estimate in their heads. Calculators and computers demand that people put in the correct information and that they know if the answers are reasonable. Usually, people look at the answer to determine if it makes sense, applying the math in their heads to the problem. This is the reason why doing math in their heads is so important to our children as they enter the 21st century.

How You Can Help

1. **Help your child do mental math with lots of small numbers in his or her head until he or she develops quick and accurate responses.** Questions such as, "If I have 4 cups, and I need 7 cups, how many more do I need?" or "If I need 12 drinks for the class, how many packages of 3 drinks will I need to buy?"

2. **Encourage your child to estimate the answer.** When estimating, try to use numbers to make it easy to solve problems quickly in your head to determine a reasonable answer. For example, when figuring 18 plus 29, an easy way to get a "close" answer is to think about 20 + 30 = [?].

3. **Allow your child to use strategies that make sense to him or her.** Ask often, "Is your answer reasonable? Is it reasonable that you added 17 and 35 and got 367? Why? Why not?"

Tips for Parents: Help Your Child with Math *(cont.)*

How You Can Help *(cont.)*

4. **Ask your child to explain how the problem was solved.** The response might help you discover if your child needs help with the procedures, the number facts, or the concepts involved. Sometimes the wrong answer to a problem might be because the child thinks the problem is asking another question. For example, when children see the problem 4 + __ = 9, they often respond with an answer of 13. They think the problem is asking "What is 4 + 9?" instead of "4 plus what missing number amount equals 9?"

   You may have learned something the teacher might find helpful. A short note or call will alert the teacher to possible ways of helping your child.

5. **Help your child be a risk taker.** Help him or her see the value of examining a wrong answer, and assure him or her that the right answers will come with proper understanding.

6. **Emphasize that math is enjoyable and practical.** Math is part of the everyday world. Even when you are at a fast-food restaurant, point to the prices on the menu and say, "Look! More numbers—they are everywhere!"

Above all, be patient. All children want to succeed. They do not want red marks or incorrect answers. They want to be proud and to make you and the teacher proud. So, the wrong answer tells you to look further, to ask questions, and to see what the wrong answer is saying about the child's understanding.

Problem-Solving Strategies

| Act it out | Draw a Picture | Use Logical Reasoning |
| Look for Patterns | Guess and Check | Make a List |

Parent Handout: Writing

Tips for Parents: Help Your Child to Write Well

Children must be ready to learn from the first day of school. And of course, preparing children for school is a historic responsibility of parents.

Should you help your child with writing? Yes, if you want your child to do well in school, enjoy self-expression, and become more self-reliant. You know how important writing will be to your child's life. It will be important from first grade through college and throughout adulthood. After all, writing is . . .

Practical —	Most of us make lists, jot down reminders, and write notes or instructions.
Job-Related —	Professional and white-collar workers write frequently—preparing memos, letters, briefing papers, sales reports, articles, research reports, or proposals. Most workers do some kind of writing on the job.
Stimulating —	Writing helps to provoke thoughts and to organize them logically and concisely.
Social —	Most of us—at least occasionally—write thank-you notes, e-mails, and letters to friends.
Therapeutic —	It can be helpful to express feelings in writing that cannot be expressed so easily by speaking.

How You Can Help

1. **Encourage your child to draw and to discuss his or her drawings.** One of the first means of communication for your child is through drawing. Ask questions such as the following: *What is the boy doing? Does the house look like ours? Can you tell me a story about this picture?*

2. **Show an interest in and ask questions about the things your child says, draws, and may try to write.** Most children's basic speech patterns are formed by the time they enter school. By that time, children speak clearly, recognize most letters of the alphabet, and may try to write.

3. **Make it real.** Your child also needs to do real writing. It is more important for the child to write a letter to a relative than it is to write a one-line note on a greeting card. Encourage your child to write to relatives and friends. Perhaps your child would enjoy corresponding with a pen pal.

Tips for Parents: Help Your Child to Write Well *(cont.)*

How You Can Help *(cont.)*

4. **Suggest note-taking.** Encourage your child to take notes on trips or outings and to describe what he or she saw. This could include a description of nature walks, a boat ride, a car trip, or other events that lend themselves to note-taking.

5. **Brainstorm.** Talk with your child as much as possible about his or her impressions and encourage the child to describe people and events to you. If the child's description is especially accurate and colorful, say so.

6. **Write together.** Have your child help you with letters, even such routine ones as ordering items from an advertisement or writing to a business firm. This helps the child to see firsthand that writing is important to adults and truly useful.

7. **Use games.** There are numerous games and puzzles that help a child to increase vocabulary and make a child more fluent in speaking and writing. Remember that building a vocabulary builds confidence. Try crossword puzzles, word games, anagrams, and cryptograms designed especially for children. Flash cards are good, too, and they are easy to make at home.

8. **Suggest making lists.** Most children like to make lists just as they like to count. Making lists is good practice and helps a child to become more organized. Boys and girls might make lists of their DVDs, CDs, baseball cards, dolls, furniture in a room, etc. They could include items they want. It is also good practice to make lists of things to do: schoolwork, dates for tests, social events, and other reminders.

9. **Encourage copying.** If a child likes a particular song, suggest learning the words by writing them down—replaying the song on your CD player or jotting down the words whenever the song is played on a radio program. Also encourage copying favorite poems or quotations from books and plays. Overall, if you show a positive and interested attitude toward writing, your child will, too.